BLS REPORTS

BLS

U.S. BUREAU OF LABOR STATISTICS

MAY 2014

REPORT 1049

Women in the Labor Force: A Databook

I0439000

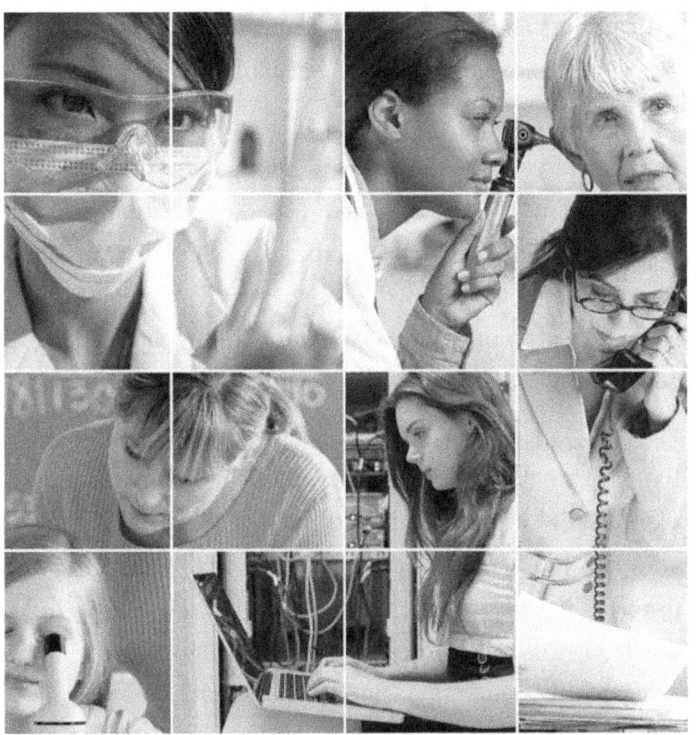

Women's participation in labor force activities has greatly expanded since the end of World War II. Immediately following the war, less than one-third of women were in the labor force. However, women soon began to participate in greater numbers, and their labor force participation rose rapidly from the 1960s through the 1980s before slowing in the 1990s. By 1999, women reached the peak of their labor force participation, 60 percent. Since then, however, labor force participation among women has declined. Nonetheless, women's labor force participation remains relatively high by historical standards, particularly among women with children, and a large share of women work full time and year round. In addition, women have increasingly attained higher levels of education: among women ages 25 to 64 who are in the labor force, the proportion with a college degree more than tripled from 1970 to 2012. Women's earnings as a proportion of men's earnings also have grown over time. In 1979, women working full time earned 62 percent of what men earned; in 2012, women's earnings were 81 percent of men's.

This report presents historical and recent labor force and earnings data for women and men from the Current Population Survey (CPS), a national monthly survey of approximately 60,000 households conducted by the U.S. Census Bureau for the U.S. Bureau of Labor Statistics. Unless otherwise noted, data are annual averages from the CPS. (For a detailed description of the source of the data and an explanation of concepts and definitions used, see the Technical Notes at the end of this report.)

Selected demographic characteristics

In 2012, 57.7 percent of women were in the labor force, down 0.4 percentage point from 2011. Men's labor force participation, which always has been much higher than that for women, also edged down in 2012, from 70.5 percent to 70.2 percent. (See tables 1 and 2.)

CONTENTS

The overall unemployment rate for women in 2012 was 7.9 percent, compared with 8.2 percent for men. Both figures were down from 2011. Women's jobless rates varied by race and ethnicity. Asian women had the lowest rate (6.1 percent), followed by White (7.0 percent), Hispanic (10.9 percent), and Black (12.8 percent) women. (See table 3.)

Labor force participation varies by marital status and differs between women and men. Among women, divorced women had the highest labor force participation rate, 66.0 percent. The rate for married women was 59.5 percent. For men, those who were married had the highest labor force participation, 74.6 percent. Divorced men had a labor force participation rate of 68.4 percent. (See table 4.)

Among mothers, the labor force participation rate was higher for those with children 6 to 17 years old than for those with younger children. In 2012, the rate for mothers with children 6 to 17 years old was 76.0 percent. The rate for those with children under 6 years old was 64.7 percent, and the rate for mothers with children under 3 years old was lower, at 60.7 percent. (See table 5; data were collected in the 2012 Annual Social and Economic Supplement to the CPS.)

Unmarried mothers have higher labor force participation rates than married mothers. In March 2012, 75.8 percent of unmarried mothers with children under 18 years old were in the labor force, compared with 68.5 percent of married mothers with children in that age range. (See table 6; data were collected in the 2012 Annual Social and Economic Supplement to the CPS.)

The labor force participation rate of all mothers with children under 18 years of age was 70.9 percent in March 2012, unchanged from a year earlier. (See tables 6 and 7; data were collected in the 2012 Annual Social and Economic Supplement to the CPS.)

Educational attainment

The educational attainment of women ages 25 to 64 in the labor force has risen substantially over the past 40 years. In 2012, 38 percent of this group held college degrees, compared with 11 percent in 1970. About 7 percent of women had less than a high school diploma (i.e., did not graduate from high school) in 2012, down from 34 percent in 1970. (See table 9.)

Occupation and industry

In 2012, women accounted for 52 percent of all workers employed in management, professional, and related occupations, somewhat more than their share of total employment (47 percent). The share of women in specific occupations within this large category varied. For example, 20 percent of software developers and 31 percent of lawyers were women, whereas 61 percent of accountants and auditors and 81 percent of elementary and middle school teachers were women. (See table 11.)

Employed Asian (47 percent) and White (43 percent) women were more likely to work in higher paying management, professional, and related occupations in 2012 than were employed Black (34 percent) and Hispanic (26 percent) women. Meanwhile, Hispanic (32 percent) and Black (28 percent) women were more likely than Asian (22 percent) and White (20 percent) women to work in lower paying service occupations. (See table 12.)

In 2012, women accounted for more than half of all workers within several industry sectors: financial activities (53 percent), education and health services (75 percent), leisure and hospitality (51 percent), and other services (52 percent). However, women were substantially underrepresented (relative to their share of total employment) in agriculture (26 percent), mining (13 percent), construction (9 percent), manufacturing (29 percent), and transportation and utilities (23 percent). (See table 14.)

Earnings

In 2012, women who worked full time in wage and salary jobs had median usual weekly earnings of $691, which represented 81 percent of men's median weekly earnings ($854). Among women, earnings were higher for Asians ($770) and Whites ($710) than for Blacks ($599) and Hispanics ($521). Women's-to-men's earnings ratios were higher for Blacks (90 percent) and Hispanics (88 percent) than for Whites (81 percent) and Asians (73 percent). (See table 16; note that the comparisons of earnings in this report are on a broad level and do not control for many factors that may be important in explaining earnings differences.)

In 2012, female full-time wage and salary workers ages 25 and older with only a high school diploma had median usual weekly earnings of $561, which represented 80 percent of the earnings of women with an associate's degree ($697) and 56 percent of the earnings of women with a bachelor's degree or higher ($1,001). (See table 17.)

Median usual weekly earnings of full-time wage and salary workers were the highest in 2012 for female pharmacists ($1,871), chief executives ($1,730), and lawyers ($1,636). (See table 18.)

Hours of work

In 2012, 26 percent of employed women usually worked part time—that is, less than 35 hours per week. In comparison, 13 percent of employed men usually worked part time. (See table 20.)

In general, employed women work fewer hours per week than men. On average, women worked 35.8 hours per week in 2012, compared with 40.8 hours for men. (See table 21.)

Of all women who worked at some point during calendar year 2011, 60 percent worked full time and year round, compared with 41 percent in 1970. For the same two years, the proportion of men who worked full time and year round rose slightly, from 66 percent in 1970 to 71 percent in 2011. (See table 22; data were collected in the 1971 and 2012 Annual Social and Economic Supplements to the CPS and reflect earnings and work experience in the previous calendar year.)

Married-couple families

Among married-couple families, 53 percent had earnings from both the wife and the husband in 2011, compared with 44 percent in 1967. Couples in which only the husband worked represented 19 percent of married-couple families in 2011, versus 36 percent in 1967. (See table 23; data

were collected in the 1968 and 2012 Annual Social and Economic Supplements to the CPS and reflect earnings and work experience in the previous calendar year.)

In 2011, working wives contributed 37 percent of their families' incomes, up by 10 percentage points from 1970, when wives' earnings accounted for 27 percent of their families' total income. The proportion of wives earning more than their husbands also has grown: in 1987, 18 percent of working wives whose husbands also worked earned more than their spouses; in 2011, the proportion was 28.1 percent. (See tables 24 and 25; data were collected in the 1971, 1988, and 2012 Annual Social and Economic Supplements to the CPS and reflect earnings and work experience in the previous calendar year.)

Minimum wage and the working poor

In 2012, 6 percent of all women paid at an hourly rate, or approximately 2.3 million women, had earnings at or below the prevailing federal minimum wage ($7.25 per hour). Among women 25 years and older who were paid at an hourly rate, 4 percent had earnings at or below the minimum wage, compared with 15 percent of women ages 16 to 24. (See table 26.)

Among workers who were in the labor force for at least 27 weeks in 2011, more women (5.5 million) than men (4.9 million) lived below the official poverty level. The working-poor rate (the ratio of the working poor to all individuals who were in the labor force for at least 27 weeks) was 8.0 percent for women and 6.2 percent for men. Black and Hispanic women were considerably more likely than White or Asian women to be among the working poor. The working-poor rates for Black and Hispanic women were 15.6 percent and 13.7 percent, respectively, compared with 6.7 percent for White women and 5.4 percent for Asian women. (See table 27; data are from the 2012 Annual Social and Economic Supplement to the CPS and reflect earnings and work experience in the previous calendar year.)

Other characteristics

Among 2012 high school graduates, young women (71 percent) were more likely than young men (61 percent) to be enrolled in college in October 2012. (See table 30; data are from the October 2012 School Enrollment Supplement to the CPS.)

Young women 16 to 24 years old who were high school dropouts were much less likely to participate in the labor force (35.5 percent) in October 2012 than those who had graduated from high school between January and October 2012 but were not enrolled in college (68.7 percent). (See table 30; data are from the October 2012 School Enrollment Supplement to the CPS.)

In October 2012, 40.5 percent of women ages 16 to 24 who were enrolled in either high school or college were in the labor force. Young men in the same age group who were enrolled in school had a lower labor force participation rate (36.1 percent). Among those not enrolled in school, women were less likely to be in the labor force than men (74.5 percent, compared with 83.6 percent). (See table 31; data are from the October 2012 School Enrollment Supplement to the CPS.)

Multiple jobholders and the self-employed

In 2012, 5.2 percent of employed women held more than one job. The rate for men was lower, at 4.6 percent. Multiple-jobholding rates for women and men have edged down in recent years and remain below the rates recorded in the mid-1990s. (See table 32.)

In 2012, 5.2 percent of working women in nonagricultural industries were self-employed, compared with 7.1 percent for their male counterparts. That same year, 40 percent of all self-employed workers were women, compared with 27 percent in 1976. (See table 33.)

Foreign born

Foreign-born women were somewhat less likely than native-born women to be in the labor force in 2012 (54.8 percent, compared with 58.2 percent). Of those in the labor force, foreign-born women were more likely to be unemployed than were native-born women (8.9 percent, as opposed to 7.7 percent). Foreign-born men were more likely to be in the labor force (78.5 percent) than native-born men (68.6 percent) and were less likely to be unemployed (7.5 percent, compared with 8.4 percent). (See table 34.)

Union membership

In 2012, 10.5 percent of female wage and salary workers were members of unions, compared with 12.0 percent of their male counterparts. For both men and women, the union membership rate in 2012 was lower than in 1983, but the rate has fallen much more for men over the 1983–2012 period. (See table 35.)

Veterans

There were 11.0 million veterans of the U.S. Armed Forces in the labor force in 2012. About 1.1 million of them, or 10 percent, were women. The unemployment rate for female veterans in 2012 was 8.3 percent. (See table 36.)

Women with disabilities

Of the 15.3 million women with disabilities in 2012, 2.6 million, or 17.1 percent, were in the labor force. Nearly half of women with disabilities were age 65 and older; labor force participation among this age group was 5.0 percent, compared with 28.9 percent among those ages 16 to 64. For women with a disability who were age 16 and older, the unemployment rate was 13.7 percent, almost twice that for women without a disability (7.7 percent). (See table 37.)

Statistical Tables

Page

Selected demographic characteristics

Educational attainment

Occupation and industry

Earnings

Hours of work

Statistical Tables continued— *Page*

Table 1. **Employment status of the civilian noninstitutional population, by age and gender, 2012 annual averages**

(Numbers in thousands)

Age	Civilian noninstitutional population	Civilian labor force						Not in labor force
		Total	Percentage of population	Employed		Unemployed		
				Total	Percentage of population	Total	Percentage of labor force	
		Total						
16 years and older	243,284	154,975	63.7	142,469	58.6	12,506	8.1	88,310
16 to 19 years	16,984	5,823	34.3	4,426	26.1	1,397	24.0	11,162
16 to 17 years.........	8,891	1,952	22.0	1,419	16.0	533	27.3	6,939
18 to 19 years.........	8,093	3,870	47.8	3,007	37.2	863	22.3	4,223
20 to 24 years...........	21,799	15,462	70.9	13,408	61.5	2,054	13.3	6,337
25 to 54 years...........	124,314	101,253	81.4	94,150	75.7	7,103	7.0	23,061
25 to 34 years.........	40,975	33,465	81.7	30,701	74.9	2,764	8.3	7,510
25 to 29 years......	20,653	16,792	81.3	15,293	74.0	1,500	8.9	3,860
30 to 34 years......	20,322	16,673	82.0	15,408	75.8	1,265	7.6	3,650
35 to 44 years.........	39,642	32,734	82.6	30,576	77.1	2,158	6.6	6,908
35 to 39 years......	19,025	15,658	82.3	14,560	76.5	1,098	7.0	3,367
40 to 44 years......	20,617	17,076	82.8	16,016	77.7	1,060	6.2	3,541
45 to 54 years.........	43,697	35,054	80.2	32,874	75.2	2,181	6.2	8,643
45 to 49 years......	21,359	17,456	81.7	16,371	76.6	1,086	6.2	3,902
50 to 54 years......	22,339	17,598	78.8	16,503	73.9	1,095	6.2	4,741
55 to 64 years...........	38,318	24,710	64.5	23,239	60.6	1,470	5.9	13,608
55 to 59 years.........	20,574	14,908	72.5	14,015	68.1	892	6.0	5,667
60 to 64 years.........	17,743	9,802	55.2	9,224	52.0	578	5.9	7,941
65 years and older......	41,869	7,727	18.5	7,245	17.3	482	6.2	34,142
65 to 69 years.........	13,801	4,427	32.1	4,133	29.9	295	6.7	9,373
70 to 74 years.........	9,853	1,917	19.5	1,794	18.2	124	6.4	7,936
75 years and older....	18,216	1,383	7.6	1,319	7.2	64	4.6	16,833

Table 1. **Employment status of the civilian noninstitutional population, by age and gender, 2012 annual averages (continued)**

(Numbers in thousands)

Age	Civilian noninstitutional population	Civilian labor force						Not in labor force
		Total	Percentage of population	Employed		Unemployed		
				Total	Percentage of population	Total	Percentage of labor force	
Women								
16 years and older	125,941	72,648	57.7	66,914	53.1	5,734	7.9	53,293
16 to 19 years	8,327	2,883	34.6	2,274	27.3	609	21.1	5,444
16 to 17 years........	4,341	1,003	23.1	760	17.5	242	24.2	3,338
18 to 19 years.........	3,986	1,880	47.2	1,514	38.0	367	19.5	2,106
20 to 24 years............	10,910	7,352	67.4	6,460	59.2	891	12.1	3,559
25 to 54 years............	63,355	47,200	74.5	43,840	69.2	3,361	7.1	16,154
25 to 34 years.........	20,770	15,382	74.1	14,094	67.9	1,288	8.4	5,388
25 to 29 years.......	10,437	7,765	74.4	7,073	67.8	692	8.9	2,672
30 to 34 years.......	10,333	7,617	73.7	7,021	67.9	597	7.8	2,716
35 to 44 years.........	20,226	15,127	74.8	14,093	69.7	1,034	6.8	5,100
35 to 39 years.......	9,716	7,156	73.7	6,630	68.2	526	7.3	2,560
40 to 44 years.......	10,510	7,970	75.8	7,462	71.0	508	6.4	2,540
45 to 54 years.........	22,358	16,692	74.7	15,653	70.0	1,039	6.2	5,667
45 to 49 years.......	10,909	8,251	75.6	7,738	70.9	513	6.2	2,658
50 to 54 years.......	11,449	8,440	73.7	7,915	69.1	525	6.2	3,009
55 to 64 years............	19,902	11,830	59.4	11,171	56.1	659	5.6	8,071
55 to 59 years.........	10,653	7,171	67.3	6,773	63.6	398	5.6	3,482
60 to 64 years.........	9,249	4,660	50.4	4,399	47.6	261	5.6	4,589
65 years and older......	23,447	3,383	14.4	3,168	13.5	214	6.3	20,064
65 to 69 years.........	7,301	2,015	27.6	1,880	25.8	135	6.7	5,286
70 to 74 years.........	5,316	821	15.4	769	14.5	52	6.4	4,495
75 years and older....	10,830	546	5.0	519	4.8	27	4.9	10,284

Table 1. **Employment status of the civilian noninstitutional population, by age and gender, 2012 annual averages (continued)**

(Numbers in thousands)

Age	Civilian noninsti- tutional population	Civilian labor force		Employed		Unemployed		Not in labor force
		Total	Percentage of population	Total	Percentage of population	Total	Percentage of labor force	
Men								
16 years and older	117,343	82,327	70.2	75,555	64.4	6,771	8.2	35,017
16 to 19 years	8,657	2,940	34.0	2,152	24.9	787	26.8	5,717
16 to 17 years.........	4,550	950	20.9	659	14.5	291	30.6	3,600
18 to 19 years.........	4,107	1,990	48.5	1,493	36.4	497	25.0	2,117
20 to 24 years............	10,889	8,110	74.5	6,948	63.8	1,163	14.3	2,778
25 to 54 years............	60,959	54,053	88.7	50,310	82.5	3,742	6.9	6,907
25 to 34 years.........	20,205	18,083	89.5	16,607	82.2	1,476	8.2	2,122
25 to 29 years......	10,216	9,027	88.4	8,219	80.5	808	9.0	1,188
30 to 34 years......	9,989	9,055	90.7	8,387	84.0	668	7.4	934
35 to 44 years.........	19,416	17,607	90.7	16,483	84.9	1,124	6.4	1,808
35 to 39 years......	9,309	8,502	91.3	7,930	85.2	572	6.7	807
40 to 44 years......	10,107	9,106	90.1	8,553	84.6	552	6.1	1,001
45 to 54 years.........	21,339	18,363	86.1	17,221	80.7	1,142	6.2	2,976
45 to 49 years......	10,449	9,205	88.1	8,633	82.6	572	6.2	1,244
50 to 54 years......	10,890	9,157	84.1	8,588	78.9	570	6.2	1,732
55 to 64 years............	18,416	12,879	69.9	12,068	65.5	811	6.3	5,537
55 to 59 years.........	9,922	7,737	78.0	7,243	73.0	494	6.4	2,185
60 to 64 years.........	8,495	5,142	60.5	4,826	56.8	317	6.2	3,352
65 years and older......	18,422	4,345	23.6	4,077	22.1	268	6.2	14,078
65 to 69 years.........	6,499	2,412	37.1	2,252	34.7	159	6.6	4,088
70 to 74 years.........	4,537	1,096	24.2	1,025	22.6	71	6.5	3,441
75 years and older...	7,386	837	11.3	800	10.8	37	4.4	6,549

Source: Current Population Survey, U.S. Bureau of Labor Statistics.

Table 2. **Employment status of the civilian noninstitutional population 16 years and older, by gender, 1948–2012 annual averages**

(Numbers in thousands)

Year	Civilian noninsti-tutional population	Civilian labor force						Not in labor force
		Total	Percentage of population	Employed		Unemployed		
				Total	Percentage of population	Total	Percentage of labor force	
				Total				
1948	103,068	60,621	58.8	58,343	56.6	2,276	3.8	42,447
1949	103,994	61,286	58.9	57,651	55.4	3,637	5.9	42,708
1950	104,995	62,208	59.2	58,918	56.1	3,288	5.3	42,787
1951	104,621	62,017	59.2	59,961	57.3	2,055	3.3	42,604
1952	105,231	62,138	59.0	60,250	57.3	1,883	3.0	43,093
1953	107,056	63,015	58.9	61,179	57.1	1,834	2.9	44,041
1954	108,321	63,643	58.8	60,109	55.5	3,532	5.5	44,678
1955	109,683	65,023	59.3	62,170	56.7	2,852	4.4	44,660
1956	110,954	66,552	60.0	63,799	57.5	2,750	4.1	44,402
1957	112,265	66,929	59.6	64,071	57.1	2,859	4.3	45,336
1958	113,727	67,639	59.5	63,036	55.4	4,602	6.8	46,088
1959	115,329	68,369	59.3	64,630	56.0	3,740	5.5	46,960
1960	117,245	69,628	59.4	65,778	56.1	3,852	5.5	47,617
1961	118,771	70,459	59.3	65,746	55.4	4,714	6.7	48,312
1962	120,153	70,614	58.8	66,702	55.5	3,911	5.5	49,539
1963	122,416	71,833	58.7	67,762	55.4	4,070	5.7	50,583
1964	124,485	73,091	58.7	69,305	55.7	3,786	5.2	51,394
1965	126,513	74,455	58.9	71,088	56.2	3,366	4.5	52,058
1966	128,058	75,770	59.2	72,895	56.9	2,875	3.8	52,288
1967	129,874	77,347	59.6	74,372	57.3	2,975	3.8	52,527
1968	132,028	78,737	59.6	75,920	57.5	2,817	3.6	53,291
1969	134,335	80,734	60.1	77,902	58.0	2,832	3.5	53,602
1970	137,085	82,771	60.4	78,678	57.5	4,093	4.9	54,315
1971	140,216	84,382	60.2	79,367	56.6	5,016	5.9	55,834
1972	144,126	87,034	60.4	82,153	57.0	4,882	5.6	57,091
1973	147,096	89,429	60.8	85,064	57.8	4,365	4.9	57,667
1974	150,120	91,949	61.3	86,794	57.8	5,156	5.6	58,171
1975	153,153	93,775	61.2	85,846	56.1	7,929	8.5	59,377
1976	156,150	96,158	61.6	88,752	56.8	7,406	7.7	59,991
1977	159,033	99,009	62.3	92,017	57.9	6,991	7.1	60,025
1978	161,910	102,251	63.2	96,048	59.3	6,202	6.1	59,659
1979	164,863	104,962	63.7	98,824	59.9	6,137	5.8	59,900
1980	167,745	106,940	63.8	99,303	59.2	7,637	7.1	60,806
1981	170,130	108,670	63.9	100,397	59.0	8,273	7.6	61,460
1982	172,271	110,204	64.0	99,526	57.8	10,678	9.7	62,067
1983	174,215	111,550	64.0	100,834	57.9	10,717	9.6	62,665
1984	176,383	113,544	64.4	105,005	59.5	8,539	7.5	62,839
1985	178,206	115,461	64.8	107,150	60.1	8,312	7.2	62,744
1986	180,587	117,834	65.3	109,597	60.7	8,237	7.0	62,752
1987	182,753	119,865	65.6	112,440	61.5	7,425	6.2	62,888
1988	184,613	121,669	65.9	114,968	62.3	6,701	5.5	62,944
1989	186,393	123,869	66.5	117,342	63.0	6,528	5.3	62,523
1990	189,164	125,840	66.5	118,793	62.8	7,047	5.6	63,324
1991	190,925	126,346	66.2	117,718	61.7	8,628	6.8	64,578

See note at end of table.

Table 2. **Employment status of the civilian noninstitutional population 16 years and older, by gender, 1948–2012 annual averages (continued)**

(Numbers in thousands)

Year	Civilian noninstitutional population	Civilian labor force						Not in labor force
		Total	Percentage of population	Employed		Unemployed		
				Total	Percentage of population	Total	Percentage of labor force	
Total								
1992	192,805	128,105	66.4	118,492	61.5	9,613	7.5	64,700
1993	194,838	129,200	66.3	120,259	61.7	8,940	6.9	65,638
1994	196,814	131,056	66.6	123,060	62.5	7,996	6.1	65,758
1995	198,584	132,304	66.6	124,900	62.9	7,404	5.6	66,280
1996	200,591	133,943	66.8	126,708	63.2	7,236	5.4	66,647
1997	203,133	136,297	67.1	129,558	63.8	6,739	4.9	66,837
1998	205,220	137,673	67.1	131,463	64.1	6,210	4.5	67,547
1999	207,753	139,368	67.1	133,488	64.3	5,880	4.2	68,385
2000	212,577	142,583	67.1	136,891	64.4	5,692	4.0	69,994
2001	215,092	143,734	66.8	136,933	63.7	6,801	4.7	71,359
2002	217,570	144,863	66.6	136,485	62.7	8,378	5.8	72,707
2003	221,168	146,510	66.2	137,736	62.3	8,774	6.0	74,658
2004	223,357	147,401	66.0	139,252	62.3	8,149	5.5	75,956
2005	226,082	149,320	66.0	141,730	62.7	7,591	5.1	76,762
2006	228,815	151,428	66.2	144,427	63.1	7,001	4.6	77,387
2007	231,867	153,124	66.0	146,047	63.0	7,078	4.6	78,743
2008	233,788	154,287	66.0	145,362	62.2	8,924	5.8	79,501
2009	235,801	154,142	65.4	139,877	59.3	14,265	9.3	81,659
2010	237,830	153,889	64.7	139,064	58.5	14,825	9.6	83,941
2011	239,618	153,617	64.1	139,869	58.4	13,747	8.9	86,001
2012	243,284	154,975	63.7	142,469	58.6	12,506	8.1	88,310
Women								
1948	53,071	17,335	32.7	16,617	31.3	717	4.1	35,737
1949	53,670	17,788	33.1	16,723	31.2	1,065	6.0	35,883
1950	54,270	18,389	33.9	17,340	32.0	1,049	5.7	35,881
1951	54,895	19,016	34.6	18,181	33.1	834	4.4	35,879
1952	55,529	19,269	34.7	18,568	33.4	698	3.6	36,261
1953	56,305	19,382	34.4	18,749	33.3	632	3.3	36,924
1954	56,925	19,678	34.6	18,490	32.5	1,188	6.0	37,247
1955	57,574	20,548	35.7	19,551	34.0	998	4.9	37,026
1956	58,228	21,461	36.9	20,419	35.1	1,039	4.8	36,769
1957	58,951	21,732	36.9	20,714	35.1	1,018	4.7	37,218
1958	59,690	22,118	37.1	20,613	34.5	1,504	6.8	37,574
1959	60,534	22,483	37.1	21,164	35.0	1,320	5.9	38,053
1960	61,582	23,240	37.7	21,874	35.5	1,366	5.9	38,343
1961	62,484	23,806	38.1	22,090	35.4	1,717	7.2	38,679
1962	63,321	24,014	37.9	22,525	35.6	1,488	6.2	39,308
1963	64,494	24,704	38.3	23,105	35.8	1,598	6.5	39,791
1964	65,637	25,412	38.7	23,831	36.3	1,581	6.2	40,225
1965	66,731	26,200	39.3	24,748	37.1	1,452	5.5	40,531
1966	67,795	27,299	40.3	25,976	38.3	1,324	4.8	40,496
1967	68,968	28,360	41.1	26,893	39.0	1,468	5.2	40,608
1968	70,179	29,204	41.6	27,807	39.6	1,397	4.8	40,976
1969	71,436	30,513	42.7	29,084	40.7	1,429	4.7	40,924

See note at end of table.

Table 2. **Employment status of the civilian noninstitutional population 16 years and older, by gender, 1948–2012 annual averages (continued)**

(Numbers in thousands)

Year	Civilian noninstitutional population	Civilian labor force						Not in labor force
		Total	Percentage of population	Employed		Unemployed		
				Total	Percentage of population	Total	Percentage of labor force	
Women								
1970	72,782	31,543	43.3	29,688	40.8	1,855	5.9	41,239
1971	74,274	32,202	43.4	29,976	40.4	2,227	6.9	42,072
1972	76,290	33,479	43.9	31,257	41.0	2,222	6.6	42,811
1973	77,804	34,804	44.7	32,715	42.0	2,089	6.0	43,000
1974	79,312	36,211	45.7	33,769	42.6	2,441	6.7	43,101
1975	80,860	37,475	46.3	33,989	42.0	3,486	9.3	43,386
1976	82,390	38,983	47.3	35,615	43.2	3,369	8.6	43,406
1977.........	83,840	40,613	48.4	37,289	44.5	3,324	8.2	43,227
1978	85,334	42,631	50.0	39,569	46.4	3,061	7.2	42,703
1979	86,843	44,235	50.9	41,217	47.5	3,018	6.8	42,608
1980	88,348	45,487	51.5	42,117	47.7	3,370	7.4	42,861
1981	89,618	46,696	52.1	43,000	48.0	3,696	7.9	42,922
1982	90,748	47,755	52.6	43,256	47.7	4,499	9.4	42,993
1983	91,684	48,503	52.9	44,047	48.0	4,457	9.2	43,181
1984	92,778	49,709	53.6	45,915	49.5	3,794	7.6	43,068
1985	93,736	51,050	54.5	47,259	50.4	3,791	7.4	42,686
1986	94,789	52,413	55.3	48,706	51.4	3,707	7.1	42,376
1987.........	95,853	53,658	56.0	50,334	52.5	3,324	6.2	42,195
1988	96,756	54,742	56.6	51,696	53.4	3,046	5.6	42,014
1989	97,630	56,030	57.4	53,027	54.3	3,003	5.4	41,601
1990	98,787	56,829	57.5	53,689	54.3	3,140	5.5	41,957
1991	99,646	57,178	57.4	53,496	53.7	3,683	6.4	42,468
1992	100,535	58,141	57.8	54,052	53.8	4,090	7.0	42,394
1993	101,506	58,795	57.9	54,910	54.1	3,885	6.6	42,711
1994	102,460	60,239	58.8	56,610	55.3	3,629	6.0	42,221
1995	103,406	60,944	58.9	57,523	55.6	3,421	5.6	42,462
1996	104,385	61,857	59.3	58,501	56.0	3,356	5.4	42,528
1997	105,418	63,036	59.8	59,873	56.8	3,162	5.0	42,382
1998	106,462	63,714	59.8	60,771	57.1	2,944	4.6	42,748
1999	108,031	64,855	60.0	62,042	57.4	2,814	4.3	43,175
2000	110,613	66,303	59.9	63,586	57.5	2,717	4.1	44,310
2001	111,811	66,848	59.8	63,737	57.0	3,111	4.7	44,962
2002	112,985	67,363	59.6	63,582	56.3	3,781	5.6	45,621
2003	114,733	68,272	59.5	64,404	56.1	3,868	5.7	46,461
2004	115,647	68,421	59.2	64,728	56.0	3,694	5.4	47,225
2005	116,931	69,288	59.3	65,757	56.2	3,531	5.1	47,643
2006	118,210	70,173	59.4	66,925	56.6	3,247	4.6	48,037
2007	119,694	70,988	59.3	67,792	56.6	3,196	4.5	48,707
2008	120,675	71,767	59.5	67,876	56.2	3,891	5.4	48,908
2009	121,665	72,019	59.2	66,208	54.4	5,811	8.1	49,646
2010	122,656	71,904	58.6	65,705	53.6	6,199	8.6	50,752
2011	123,300	71,642	58.1	65,579	53.2	6,063	8.5	51,658
2012	125,941	72,648	57.7	66,914	53.1	5,734	7.9	53,293

See note at end of table.

Table 2. **Employment status of the civilian noninstitutional population 16 years and older, by gender, 1948–2012 annual averages (continued)**

(Numbers in thousands)

Year	Civilian noninsti-tutional population	Civilian labor force						Not in labor force
		Total	Percentage of population	Employed		Unemployed		
				Total	Percentage of population	Total	Percentage of labor force	
				Men				
1948	49,996	43,286	86.6	41,725	83.5	1,559	3.6	6,710
1949	50,321	43,498	86.4	40,925	81.3	2,572	5.9	6,825
1950	50,725	43,819	86.4	41,578	82.0	2,239	5.1	6,906
1951	49,727	43,001	86.3	41,780	84.0	1,221	2.8	6,725
1952	49,700	42,869	86.3	41,682	83.9	1,185	2.8	6,832
1953	50,750	43,633	86.0	42,430	83.6	1,202	2.8	7,117
1954	51,395	43,965	85.5	41,619	81.0	2,344	5.3	7,431
1955	52,109	44,475	85.4	42,621	81.8	1,854	4.2	7,634
1956	52,723	45,091	85.5	43,379	82.3	1,711	3.8	7,633
1957	53,315	45,197	84.8	43,357	81.3	1,841	4.1	8,118
1958	54,033	45,521	84.2	42,423	78.5	3,098	6.8	8,514
1959	54,793	45,886	83.7	43,466	79.3	2,420	5.2	8,907
1960	55,662	46,388	83.3	43,904	78.9	2,486	5.4	9,274
1961	56,286	46,653	82.9	43,656	77.6	2,997	6.4	9,633
1962	56,831	46,600	82.0	44,177	77.7	2,423	5.2	10,231
1963	57,921	47,129	81.4	44,657	77.1	2,472	5.2	10,792
1964	58,847	47,679	81.0	45,474	77.3	2,205	4.6	11,169
1965	59,782	48,255	80.7	46,340	77.5	1,914	4.0	11,527
1966	60,262	48,471	80.4	46,919	77.9	1,551	3.2	11,792
1967	60,905	48,987	80.4	47,479	78.0	1,508	3.1	11,919
1968	61,847	49,533	80.1	48,114	77.8	1,419	2.9	12,315
1969	62,898	50,221	79.8	48,818	77.6	1,403	2.8	12,677
1970	64,304	51,228	79.7	48,990	76.2	2,238	4.4	13,076
1971	65,942	52,180	79.1	49,390	74.9	2,789	5.3	13,762
1972	67,835	53,555	78.9	50,896	75.0	2,659	5.0	14,280
1973	69,292	54,624	78.8	52,349	75.5	2,275	4.2	14,667
1974	70,808	55,739	78.7	53,024	74.9	2,714	4.9	15,069
1975	72,291	56,299	77.9	51,857	71.7	4,442	7.9	15,993
1976	73,759	57,174	77.5	53,138	72.0	4,036	7.1	16,585
1977.........	75,193	58,396	77.7	54,728	72.8	3,667	6.3	16,797
1978	76,576	59,620	77.9	56,479	73.8	3,142	5.3	16,956
1979	78,020	60,726	77.8	57,607	73.8	3,120	5.1	17,293
1980	79,398	61,453	77.4	57,186	72.0	4,267	6.9	17,945
1981	80,511	61,974	77.0	57,397	71.3	4,577	7.4	18,537
1982	81,523	62,450	76.6	56,271	69.0	6,179	9.9	19,073
1983	82,531	63,047	76.4	56,787	68.8	6,260	9.9	19,484
1984	83,605	63,835	76.4	59,091	70.7	4,744	7.4	19,771
1985	84,469	64,411	76.3	59,891	70.9	4,521	7.0	20,058
1986	85,798	65,422	76.3	60,892	71.0	4,530	6.9	20,376
1987.........	86,899	66,207	76.2	62,107	71.5	4,101	6.2	20,692
1988	87,857	66,927	76.2	63,273	72.0	3,655	5.5	20,930
1989	88,762	67,840	76.4	64,315	72.5	3,525	5.2	20,923
1990	90,377	69,011	76.4	65,104	72.0	3,906	5.7	21,367
1991	91,278	69,168	75.8	64,223	70.4	4,946	7.2	22,110
1992	92,270	69,964	75.8	64,440	69.8	5,523	7.9	22,306

See note at end of table.

Table 2. **Employment status of the civilian noninstitutional population 16 years and older, by gender, 1948–2012 annual averages (continued)**

(Numbers in thousands)

Year	Civilian noninsti-tutional population	Civilian labor force						Not in labor force
		Total	Percentage of population	Employed		Unemployed		
				Total	Percentage of population	Total	Percentage of labor force	
				Men				
1993	93,332	70,404	75.4	65,349	70.0	5,055	7.2	22,927
1994	94,355	70,817	75.1	66,450	70.4	4,367	6.2	23,538
1995	95,178	71,360	75.0	67,377	70.8	3,983	5.6	23,818
1996	96,206	72,087	74.9	68,207	70.9	3,880	5.4	24,119
1997	97,715	73,261	75.0	69,685	71.3	3,577	4.9	24,454
1998	98,758	73,959	74.9	70,693	71.6	3,266	4.4	24,799
1999	99,722	74,512	74.7	71,446	71.6	3,066	4.1	25,210
2000	101,964	76,280	74.8	73,305	71.9	2,975	3.9	25,684
2001	103,282	76,886	74.4	73,196	70.9	3,690	4.8	26,396
2002	104,585	77,500	74.1	72,903	69.7	4,597	5.9	27,085
2003	106,435	78,238	73.5	73,332	68.9	4,906	6.3	28,197
2004	107,710	78,980	73.3	74,524	69.2	4,456	5.6	28,730
2005	109,151	80,033	73.3	75,973	69.6	4,059	5.1	29,119
2006	110,605	81,255	73.5	77,502	70.1	3,753	4.6	29,350
2007	112,173	82,136	73.2	78,254	69.8	3,882	4.7	30,036
2008	113,113	82,520	73.0	77,486	68.5	5,033	6.1	30,593
2009	114,136	82,123	72.0	73,670	64.5	8,453	10.3	32,013
2010	115,174	81,985	71.2	73,359	63.7	8,626	10.5	33,189
2011	116,317	81,975	70.5	74,290	63.9	7,684	9.4	34,343
2012	117,343	82,327	70.2	75,555	64.4	6,771	8.2	35,017

Note: Revisions to population controls and other changes can affect the comparability of labor force levels over time. In recent years, for example, updated population controls have been introduced annually with the release of January data. Information about historical comparability is online at www.bls.gov/cps/documentation.htm#comp.

Source: Current Population Survey, U.S. Bureau of Labor Statistics.

Table 3. **Employment status, by race, age, gender, and Hispanic or Latino ethnicity, 2012 annual averages**

(Numbers in thousands)

Race, age, gender, and Hispanic or Latino ethnicity	Civilian noninstitutional population	Civilian labor force						Not in labor force
		Total	Percentage of population	Employed		Unemployed		
				Total	Percentage of population	Total	Percentage of labor force	
White								
Total, 16 years and older......	193,204	123,684	64.0	114,769	59.4	8,915	7.2	69,520
16 to 19 years.................	12,658	4,669	36.9	3,665	29.0	1,004	21.5	7,988
20 to 24 years.................	16,289	11,914	73.1	10,561	64.8	1,353	11.4	4,375
25 to 54 years.................	96,774	79,635	82.3	74,626	77.1	5,009	6.3	17,139
55 to 64 years.................	31,511	20,752	65.9	19,608	62.2	1,144	5.5	10,759
65 years and older...........	35,973	6,714	18.7	6,309	17.5	405	6.0	29,259
Women, 16 years and older..	98,938	56,763	57.4	52,779	53.3	3,985	7.0	42,175
16 to 19 years.................	6,172	2,288	37.1	1,868	30.3	420	18.4	3,884
20 to 24 years.................	8,078	5,575	69.0	5,014	62.1	561	10.1	2,503
25 to 54 years.................	48,532	36,240	74.7	33,925	69.9	2,314	6.4	12,292
55 to 64 years.................	16,179	9,782	60.5	9,274	57.3	508	5.2	6,397
65 years and older...........	19,978	2,879	14.4	2,698	13.5	181	6.3	17,099
Men, 16 years and older......	94,266	66,921	71.0	61,990	65.8	4,931	7.4	27,345
16 to 19 years.................	6,486	2,382	36.7	1,797	27.7	584	24.5	4,104
20 to 24 years.................	8,211	6,339	77.2	5,547	67.6	792	12.5	1,872
25 to 54 years.................	48,242	43,395	90.0	40,701	84.4	2,694	6.2	4,847
55 to 64 years.................	15,333	10,970	71.6	10,334	67.4	637	5.8	4,362
65 years and older...........	15,995	3,835	24.0	3,611	22.6	224	5.8	12,160
Black or African American								
Total, 16 years and older......	29,907	18,400	61.5	15,856	53.0	2,544	13.8	11,508
16 to 19 years.................	2,643	711	26.9	438	16.6	272	38.3	1,932
20 to 24 years.................	3,326	2,210	66.5	1,700	51.1	510	23.1	1,115
25 to 54 years.................	16,008	12,510	78.1	11,016	68.8	1,494	11.9	3,498
55 to 64 years.................	4,281	2,369	55.3	2,161	50.5	209	8.8	1,912
65 years and older...........	3,650	599	16.4	540	14.8	59	9.8	3,051
Women, 16 years and older..	16,400	9,805	59.8	8,553	52.2	1,252	12.8	6,595
16 to 19 years.................	1,324	373	28.2	240	18.1	133	35.6	951
20 to 24 years.................	1,740	1,157	66.5	916	52.6	241	20.8	583
25 to 54 years.................	8,777	6,687	76.2	5,933	67.6	754	11.3	2,090
55 to 64 years.................	2,358	1,271	53.9	1,173	49.7	98	7.7	1,087
65 years and older...........	2,201	317	14.4	291	13.2	26	8.2	1,884
Men, 16 years and older......	13,508	8,594	63.6	7,302	54.1	1,292	15.0	4,913
16 to 19 years.................	1,319	338	25.6	198	15.1	140	41.3	981
20 to 24 years.................	1,586	1,054	66.4	784	49.5	269	25.6	532
25 to 54 years.................	7,231	5,823	80.5	5,082	70.3	740	12.7	1,408
55 to 64 years.................	1,923	1,099	57.1	988	51.4	110	10.1	825
65 years and older...........	1,449	281	19.4	249	17.2	32	11.5	1,168

See note at end of table.

Table 3. **Employment status, by race, age, gender, and Hispanic or Latino ethnicity, 2012 annual averages (continued)**

(Numbers in thousands)

Race, age, gender, and Hispanic or Latino ethnicity	Civilian noninstitutional population	Civilian labor force						Not in labor force
		Total	Percentage of population	Employed		Unemployed		
				Total	Percentage of population	Total	Percentage of labor force	
Asian								
Total, 16 years and older......	12,815	8,188	63.9	7,705	60.1	483	5.9	4,627
16 to 19 years.................	802	162	20.1	128	15.9	34	20.8	640
20 to 24 years.................	1,151	608	52.8	544	47.3	64	10.5	543
25 to 54 years.................	7,526	5,978	79.4	5,679	75.5	300	5.0	1,547
55 to 64 years.................	1,719	1,144	66.5	1,071	62.3	73	6.4	575
65 years and older...........	1,617	296	18.3	283	17.5	12	4.2	1,321
Women, 16 years and older..	6,815	3,853	56.5	3,620	53.1	234	6.1	2,962
16 to 19 years.................	391	85	21.7	69	17.5	16	19.0	306
20 to 24 years.................	575	280	48.7	250	43.4	31	10.9	295
25 to 54 years.................	3,994	2,799	70.1	2,652	66.4	148	5.3	1,194
55 to 64 years.................	947	563	59.5	528	55.8	35	6.3	384
65 years and older...........	909	126	13.9	122	13.4	4	3.2	783
Men, 16 years and older......	6,000	4,334	72.2	4,085	68.1	249	5.8	1,666
16 to 19 years.................	411	77	18.7	59	14.4	18	22.8	334
20 to 24 years.................	576	328	57.0	295	51.1	34	10.2	248
25 to 54 years.................	3,532	3,179	90.0	3,027	85.7	152	4.8	353
55 to 64 years.................	772	580	75.2	543	70.3	38	6.5	192
65 years and older...........	708	170	23.9	161	22.8	8	4.9	539
Hispanic or Latino ethnicity								
Total, 16 years and older......	36,759	24,391	66.4	21,878	59.5	2,514	10.3	12,368
16 to 19 years.................	3,656	1,131	30.9	808	22.1	324	28.6	2,524
20 to 24 years.................	4,502	3,205	71.2	2,761	61.3	444	13.8	1,297
25 to 54 years.................	21,894	17,358	79.3	15,858	72.4	1,500	8.6	4,536
55 to 64 years.................	3,613	2,185	60.5	1,983	54.9	201	9.2	1,428
65 years and older...........	3,094	512	16.5	467	15.1	44	8.7	2,582
Women, 16 years and older..	18,324	10,365	56.6	9,235	50.4	1,130	10.9	7,959
16 to 19 years.................	1,776	512	28.8	377	21.2	135	26.4	1,265
20 to 24 years.................	2,161	1,368	63.3	1,178	54.5	190	13.9	794
25 to 54 years.................	10,738	7,284	67.8	6,582	61.3	702	9.6	3,454
55 to 64 years.................	1,884	969	51.4	887	47.1	83	8.5	915
65 years and older...........	1,765	232	13.2	212	12.0	20	8.8	1,533
Men, 16 years and older......	18,434	14,026	76.1	12,643	68.6	1,383	9.9	4,408
16 to 19 years.................	1,879	620	33.0	431	22.9	189	30.5	1,259
20 to 24 years.................	2,341	1,837	78.5	1,584	67.6	254	13.8	504
25 to 54 years.................	11,157	10,074	90.3	9,276	83.1	798	7.9	1,083
55 to 64 years.................	1,729	1,215	70.3	1,097	63.4	119	9.8	513
65 years and older...........	1,329	280	21.1	256	19.2	24	8.6	1,049

Note: Estimates for the race groups shown (White, Black or African American, and Asian) do not sum to totals because data are not presented for all races. Persons whose ethnicity is identified as Hispanic or Latino may be of any race.
Source: Current Population Survey, U.S. Bureau of Labor Statistics.

Table 4. **Employment status, by marital status and gender, 2012 annual averages**

(Numbers in thousands)

Marital status and gender	Civilian noninstitutional population	Civilian labor force						Not in labor force
		Total	Percentage of population	Employed		Unemployed		
				Total	Percentage of population	Total	Percentage of labor force	
Total								
Total, 16 years and older............	243,284	154,975	63.7	142,469	58.6	12,506	8.1	88,310
Married, spouse present...........	122,977	82,530	67.1	78,341	63.7	4,189	5.1	38,321
Unmarried, total....................	120,308	72,444	60.2	64,128	53.3	8,316	11.5	43,431
Never married....................	72,447	47,000	64.9	40,974	56.6	6,026	12.8	22,235
Other marital status..............	47,861	25,444	53.2	23,154	48.4	2,291	9.0	21,196
Divorced.........................	24,869	16,675	67.1	15,229	61.2	1,446	8.7	7,538
Separated........................	8,790	5,887	67.0	5,263	59.9	624	10.6	2,606
Widowed.........................	14,202	2,882	20.3	2,662	18.7	220	7.6	11,052
Women								
Total, 16 years and older............	125,941	72,648	57.7	66,914	53.1	5,734	7.9	53,293
Married, spouse present...........	61,219	36,436	59.5	34,521	56.4	1,915	5.3	24,783
Unmarried, total....................	64,722	36,212	56.0	32,393	50.0	3,819	10.5	28,510
Never married....................	34,267	21,506	62.8	18,973	55.4	2,533	11.8	12,761
Other marital status..............	30,454	14,706	48.3	13,420	44.1	1,286	8.7	15,748
Divorced.........................	14,233	9,397	66.0	8,625	60.6	772	8.2	4,836
Separated........................	4,955	3,154	63.7	2,803	56.6	351	11.1	1,800
Widowed.........................	11,266	2,155	19.1	1,993	17.7	162	7.5	9,112
Men								
Total, 16 years and older............	117,343	82,327	70.2	75,555	64.4	6,771	8.2	35,017
Married, spouse present...........	61,757	46,094	74.6	43,820	71.0	2,274	4.9	14,811
Unmarried, total....................	55,586	36,232	65.2	31,735	57.1	4,497	12.4	17,178
Never married....................	38,180	25,494	66.8	22,002	57.6	3,492	13.7	10,972
Other marital status..............	17,406	10,738	61.7	9,734	55.9	1,005	9.4	6,206
Divorced.........................	10,635	7,278	68.4	6,604	62.1	674	9.3	3,076
Separated........................	3,836	2,733	71.2	2,460	64.1	273	10.0	983
Widowed.........................	2,935	728	24.8	669	22.8	58	8.0	2,147

Source: Current Population Survey, U.S. Bureau of Labor Statistics.

Table 5. Employment status, by gender, presence and age of children, race, and Hispanic or Latino ethnicity, March 2012

(Numbers in thousands)

Characteristic	Civilian noninstitutional population	Civilian labor force						Not in labor force
		Total	Percentage of population	Employed		Unemployed		
				Total	Percentage of population	Total	Percentage of labor force	
Total								
Women, 16 years and older..............	125,619	72,606	57.8	66,860	53.2	5,745	7.9	53,013
With children under 18 years old.......	35,822	25,384	70.9	23,366	65.2	2,018	7.9	10,438
With children 6 to 17, none younger..	19,645	14,922	76.0	13,908	70.8	1,014	6.8	4,724
With children under 6 years old.......	16,177	10,462	64.7	9,458	58.5	1,004	9.6	5,714
With children under 3 years old......	9,106	5,529	60.7	4,960	54.5	569	10.3	3,577
With no children under 18 years old...	89,797	47,222	52.6	43,494	48.4	3,728	7.9	42,575
Men, 16 years and older..................	116,984	81,607	69.8	74,109	63.4	7,498	9.2	35,376
With children under 18 years old.......	26,771	24,980	93.3	23,534	87.9	1,445	5.8	1,791
With children 6 to 17, none younger..	14,897	13,763	92.4	12,977	87.1	786	5.7	1,134
With children under 6 years old.......	11,874	11,217	94.5	10,557	88.9	659	5.9	657
With children under 3 years old......	6,778	6,432	94.9	6,053	89.3	378	5.9	346
With no children under 18 years old...	90,213	56,627	62.8	50,575	56.1	6,052	10.7	33,585
White								
Women, 16 years and older..............	98,752	56,703	57.4	52,744	53.4	3,958	7.0	42,049
With children under 18 years old.......	27,349	19,301	70.6	17,969	65.7	1,333	6.9	8,047
With children 6 to 17, none younger..	15,081	11,402	75.6	10,721	71.1	681	6.0	3,679
With children under 6 years old.......	12,268	7,899	64.4	7,248	59.1	652	8.2	4,369
With children under 3 years old......	6,981	4,219	60.4	3,849	55.1	371	8.8	2,762
With no children under 18 years old...	71,403	37,401	52.4	34,775	48.7	2,626	7.0	34,002
Men, 16 years and older..................	94,146	66,592	70.7	61,097	64.9	5,495	8.3	27,554
With children under 18 years old.......	21,758	20,431	93.9	19,366	89.0	1,065	5.2	1,327
With children 6 to 17, none younger..	12,150	11,291	92.9	10,702	88.1	589	5.2	859
With children under 6 years old.......	9,608	9,140	95.1	8,664	90.2	476	5.2	468
With children under 3 years old......	5,488	5,229	95.3	4,964	90.5	265	5.1	259
With no children under 18 years old...	72,388	46,162	63.8	41,731	57.6	4,430	9.6	26,227
Black or African American								
Women, 16 years and older..............	16,343	9,825	60.1	8,557	52.4	1,267	12.9	6,518
With children under 18 years old.......	5,087	3,829	75.3	3,300	64.9	529	13.8	1,258
With children 6 to 17, none younger..	2,769	2,221	80.2	1,973	71.2	248	11.2	548
With children under 6 years old.......	2,318	1,608	69.4	1,327	57.3	281	17.5	710
With children under 3 years old......	1,244	818	65.7	663	53.3	155	18.9	427
With no children under 18 years old...	11,255	5,996	53.3	5,258	46.7	738	12.3	5,260
Men, 16 years and older..................	13,447	8,400	62.5	7,040	52.4	1,360	16.2	5,047
With children under 18 years old.......	2,454	2,180	88.8	1,959	79.9	220	10.1	274
With children 6 to 17, none younger..	1,381	1,211	87.7	1,106	80.0	106	8.7	170
With children under 6 years old.......	1,072	968	90.3	854	79.6	114	11.8	104
With children under 3 years old......	599	550	91.8	482	80.6	67	12.3	49
With no children under 18 years old...	10,993	6,220	56.6	5,080	46.2	1,140	18.3	4,773

See note at end of table.

Table 5. **Employment status, by gender, presence and age of children, race, and Hispanic or Latino ethnicity, March 2012 (continued)**

(Numbers in thousands)

Characteristic	Civilian noninsti-tutional population	Civilian labor force						Not in labor force
		Total	Percentage of population	Employed		Unemployed		
				Total	Percentage of population	Total	Percentage of labor force	
Asian								
Women, 16 years and older...............	6,834	3,864	56.5	3,649	53.4	215	5.6	2,970
With children under 18 years old........	2,203	1,400	63.6	1,343	61.0	57	4.1	803
With children 6 to 17, none younger..	1,183	821	69.4	793	67.1	28	3.4	361
With children under 6 years old........	1,021	579	56.7	550	53.9	29	5.0	441
With children under 3 years old......	571	299	52.3	280	49.0	19	6.3	272
With no children under 18 years old...	4,631	2,464	53.2	2,306	49.8	158	6.4	2,167
Men, 16 years and older...................	5,979	4,284	71.7	3,969	66.4	315	7.4	1,694
With children under 18 years old........	1,801	1,672	92.9	1,563	86.8	110	6.6	128
With children 6 to 17, none younger..	960	891	92.8	822	85.6	69	7.7	69
With children under 6 years old........	841	781	92.9	741	88.1	41	5.2	59
With children under 3 years old......	498	469	94.2	437	87.8	32	6.8	29
With no children under 18 years old...	4,178	2,612	62.5	2,407	57.6	205	7.9	1,566
Hispanic or Latino ethnicity								
Women, 16 years and older...............	18,185	10,378	57.1	9,293	51.1	1,086	10.5	7,807
With children under 18 years old........	7,500	4,803	64.0	4,290	57.2	512	10.7	2,698
With children 6 to 17, none younger..	3,732	2,617	70.1	2,359	63.2	258	9.9	1,115
With children under 6 years old........	3,768	2,186	58.0	1,932	51.3	254	11.6	1,582
With children under 3 years old......	2,073	1,089	52.5	949	45.8	140	12.9	984
With no children under 18 years old...	10,685	5,576	52.2	5,002	46.8	573	10.3	5,109
Men, 16 years and older...................	18,276	13,676	74.8	12,168	66.6	1,508	11.0	4,599
With children under 18 years old........	5,175	4,775	92.3	4,407	85.2	368	7.7	400
With children 6 to 17, none younger..	2,633	2,391	90.8	2,198	83.5	193	8.1	242
With children under 6 years old........	2,542	2,384	93.8	2,209	86.9	175	7.4	158
With children under 3 years old......	1,435	1,360	94.8	1,261	87.9	99	7.3	75
With no children under 18 years old...	13,101	8,901	67.9	7,761	59.2	1,140	12.8	4,200

Note: Children are parents' "own" children and are sons, daughters, stepchildren, or adopted children. Not included are nieces, nephews, grandchildren, and other related and unrelated children. Estimates for the race groups shown (White, Black or African American, and Asian) do not sum to totals because data are not presented for all races. Persons whose ethnicity is identified as Hispanic or Latino may be of any race.

Source: 2012 Annual Social and Economic Supplement, Current Population Survey, U.S. Bureau of Labor Statistics.

Table 6. **Employment status of women, by presence and age of youngest child, marital status, race, and Hispanic or Latino ethnicity, March 2012**

(Numbers in thousands)

Presence and age of children	Civilian noninsti-tutional population	Civilian labor force						Not in labor force
		Total	Percentage of population	Employed		Unemployed		
				Total	Percentage of population	Total	Percentage of labor force	
Total, all marital statuses								
Total women, 16 years and older............	125,619	72,606	57.8	66,860	53.2	5,745	7.9	53,013
With children under 18 years old...........	35,822	25,384	70.9	23,366	65.2	2,018	7.9	10,438
With children 6 to 17 years old, none younger..............................	19,645	14,922	76.0	13,908	70.8	1,014	6.8	4,724
With children under 6 years old...........	16,177	10,462	64.7	9,458	58.5	1,004	9.6	5,714
With children under 3 years old.........	9,106	5,529	60.7	4,960	54.5	569	10.3	3,577
With no children under 18 years old.......	89,797	47,222	52.6	43,494	48.4	3,728	7.9	42,575
Total, married, spouse present								
Total women, 16 years and older............	61,011	36,363	59.6	34,423	56.4	1,940	5.3	24,648
With children under 18 years old...........	24,430	16,746	68.5	15,887	65.0	859	5.1	7,684
With children 6 to 17 years old, none younger..............................	13,390	9,868	73.7	9,397	70.2	471	4.8	3,521
With children under 6 years old...........	11,041	6,878	62.3	6,491	58.8	387	5.6	4,163
With children under 3 years old.........	6,324	3,744	59.2	3,527	55.8	218	5.8	2,580
With no children under 18 years old.......	36,580	19,617	53.6	18,536	50.7	1,081	5.5	16,963
Total, other marital statuses[1]								
Total women, 16 years and older............	64,608	36,243	56.1	32,437	50.2	3,805	10.5	28,365
With children under 18 years old...........	11,392	8,638	75.8	7,479	65.7	1,159	13.4	2,754
With children 6 to 17 years old, none younger..............................	6,256	5,053	80.8	4,511	72.1	542	10.7	1,202
With children under 6 years old...........	5,136	3,584	69.8	2,968	57.8	617	17.2	1,552
With children under 3 years old.........	2,782	1,785	64.2	1,434	51.5	351	19.7	997
With no children under 18 years old.......	53,216	27,605	51.9	24,959	46.9	2,646	9.6	25,611
White, all marital statuses								
Total women, 16 years and older............	98,752	56,703	57.4	52,744	53.4	3,958	7.0	42,049
With children under 18 years old...........	27,349	19,301	70.6	17,969	65.7	1,333	6.9	8,047
With children 6 to 17 years old, none younger..............................	15,081	11,402	75.6	10,721	71.1	681	6.0	3,679
With children under 6 years old...........	12,268	7,899	64.4	7,248	59.1	652	8.2	4,369
With children under 3 years old.........	6,981	4,219	60.4	3,849	55.1	371	8.8	2,762
With no children under 18 years old.......	71,403	37,401	52.4	34,775	48.7	2,626	7.0	34,002
White, married, spouse present								
Total women, 16 years and older............	51,304	30,332	59.1	28,769	56.1	1,563	5.2	20,972
With children under 18 years old...........	19,969	13,687	68.5	13,001	65.1	686	5.0	6,282
With children 6 to 17 years old, none younger..............................	10,998	8,108	73.7	7,729	70.3	380	4.7	2,889
With children under 6 years old...........	8,971	5,579	62.2	5,272	58.8	307	5.5	3,392
With children under 3 years old.........	5,169	3,059	59.2	2,888	55.9	171	5.6	2,110
With no children under 18 years old.......	31,335	16,645	53.1	15,768	50.3	877	5.3	14,690
White, other marital statuses[1]								
Total women, 16 years and older............	47,448	26,371	55.6	23,975	50.5	2,395	9.1	21,077
With children under 18 years old...........	7,380	5,614	76.1	4,968	67.3	646	11.5	1,766
With children 6 to 17 years old, none younger..............................	4,083	3,294	80.7	2,993	73.3	301	9.1	790
With children under 6 years old...........	3,297	2,321	70.4	1,976	59.9	345	14.9	976
With children under 3 years old.........	1,812	1,160	64.0	961	53.0	200	17.2	652
With no children under 18 years old.......	40,068	20,756	51.8	19,007	47.4	1,749	8.4	19,312

See footnote at end of table.

Table 6. **Employment status of women, by presence and age of youngest child, marital status, race, and Hispanic or Latino ethnicity, March 2012 (continued)**

(Numbers in thousands)

Presence and age of children	Civilian noninsti- tutional population	Civilian labor force						Not in labor force
		Total	Percentage of population	Employed		Unemployed		
				Total	Percentage of population	Total	Percentage of labor force	
Black or African American, all marital statuses								
Total women, 16 years and older............	16,343	9,825	60.1	8,557	52.4	1,267	12.9	6,518
With children under 18 years old............	5,087	3,829	75.3	3,300	64.9	529	13.8	1,258
With children 6 to 17 years old, none younger.................	2,769	2,221	80.2	1,973	71.2	248	11.2	548
With children under 6 years old............	2,318	1,608	69.4	1,327	57.3	281	17.5	710
With children under 3 years old.........	1,244	818	65.7	663	53.3	155	18.9	427
With no children under 18 years old.......	11,255	5,996	53.3	5,258	46.7	738	12.3	5,260
Black or African American, married, spouse present								
Total women, 16 years and older............	4,373	2,865	65.5	2,668	61.0	197	6.9	1,509
With children under 18 years old............	1,883	1,422	75.5	1,328	70.5	94	6.6	460
With children 6 to 17 years old, none younger.................	1,040	820	78.8	774	74.4	46	5.6	220
With children under 6 years old............	843	603	71.5	555	65.8	48	8.0	240
With children under 3 years old.........	471	324	68.8	294	62.5	30	9.2	147
With no children under 18 years old.......	2,490	1,442	57.9	1,340	53.8	103	7.1	1,048
Black or African American, other marital statuses[1]								
Total women, 16 years and older............	11,969	6,960	58.2	5,890	49.2	1,071	15.4	5,009
With children under 18 years old............	3,204	2,407	75.1	1,972	61.5	435	18.1	798
With children 6 to 17 years old, none younger.................	1,730	1,402	81.0	1,199	69.3	203	14.5	328
With children under 6 years old............	1,474	1,005	68.2	773	52.4	233	23.1	469
With children under 3 years old.........	774	494	63.8	369	47.7	125	25.3	280
With no children under 18 years old.......	8,765	4,554	52.0	3,918	44.7	635	14.0	4,211
Asian, all marital statuses								
Total women, 16 years and older............	6,834	3,864	56.5	3,649	53.4	215	5.6	2,970
With children under 18 years old............	2,203	1,400	63.6	1,343	61.0	57	4.1	803
With children 6 to 17 years old, none younger.................	1,183	821	69.4	793	67.1	28	3.4	361
With children under 6 years old............	1,021	579	56.7	550	53.9	29	5.0	441
With children under 3 years old.........	571	299	52.3	280	49.0	19	6.3	272
With no children under 18 years old.......	4,631	2,464	53.2	2,306	49.8	158	6.4	2,167
Asian, married, spouse present								
Total women, 16 years and older............	3,990	2,312	58.0	2,211	55.4	101	4.4	1,677
With children under 18 years old............	1,899	1,157	60.9	1,123	59.1	34	3.0	742
With children 6 to 17 years old, none younger.................	1,003	674	67.2	658	65.6	16	2.4	329
With children under 6 years old............	896	483	53.9	465	51.8	18	3.8	413
With children under 3 years old.........	504	249	49.3	239	47.5	9	3.7	255
With no children under 18 years old.......	2,090	1,155	55.3	1,089	52.1	66	5.7	935
Asian, other marital statuses[1]								
Total women, 16 years and older............	2,845	1,552	54.6	1,437	50.5	115	7.4	1,293
With children under 18 years old............	304	244	80.2	220	72.5	23	9.5	60
With children 6 to 17 years old, none younger.................	180	147	82.0	135	75.3	12	8.3	32
With children under 6 years old............	124	96	77.4	85	68.6	11	11.4	28
With children under 3 years old.........	68	51	75.0	41	60.6	10	19.1	17
With no children under 18 years old.......	2,541	1,308	51.5	1,217	47.9	92	7.0	1,232

See footnote at end of table.

Table 6. **Employment status of women, by presence and age of youngest child, marital status, race, and Hispanic or Latino ethnicity, March 2012 (continued)**

(Numbers in thousands)

Presence and age of children	Civilian noninstitutional population	Civilian labor force						Not in labor force
		Total	Percentage of population	Employed		Unemployed		
				Total	Percentage of population	Total	Percentage of labor force	
Hispanic or Latino ethnicity, all marital statuses								
Total women, 16 years and older.............	18,185	10,378	57.1	9,293	51.1	1,086	10.5	7,807
With children under 18 years old............	7,500	4,803	64.0	4,290	57.2	512	10.7	2,698
With children 6 to 17 years old, none younger...............................	3,732	2,617	70.1	2,359	63.2	258	9.9	1,115
With children under 6 years old............	3,768	2,186	58.0	1,932	51.3	254	11.6	1,582
With children under 3 years old..........	2,073	1,089	52.5	949	45.8	140	12.9	984
With no children under 18 years old.......	10,685	5,576	52.2	5,002	46.8	573	10.3	5,109
Hispanic or Latino ethnicity, married, spouse present								
Total women, 16 years and older.............	8,106	4,577	56.5	4,193	51.7	384	8.4	3,528
With children under 18 years old............	4,751	2,797	58.9	2,558	53.8	239	8.6	1,954
With children 6 to 17 years old, none younger...............................	2,411	1,577	65.4	1,438	59.6	140	8.9	834
With children under 6 years old............	2,341	1,220	52.1	1,120	47.9	100	8.2	1,121
With children under 3 years old..........	1,282	610	47.6	549	42.9	61	10.0	671
With no children under 18 years old.......	3,354	1,780	53.1	1,636	48.8	144	8.1	1,574
Hispanic or Latino ethnicity, other marital statuses[1]								
Total women, 16 years and older.............	10,080	5,801	57.6	5,099	50.6	702	12.1	4,278
With children under 18 years old............	2,749	2,006	73.0	1,733	63.0	273	13.6	743
With children 6 to 17 years old, none younger...............................	1,321	1,039	78.7	921	69.7	118	11.4	282
With children under 6 years old............	1,428	966	67.7	812	56.8	155	16.0	462
With children under 3 years old..........	792	479	60.5	400	50.5	79	16.5	313
With no children under 18 years old.......	7,331	3,796	51.8	3,367	45.9	429	11.3	3,535

[1] Includes never-married, divorced, separated, and widowed women.

Note: Children are parents' "own" children and are sons, daughters, stepchildren, or adopted children. Not included are nieces, nephews, grandchildren, and other related and unrelated children. Details for the race groups shown (White, Black or African American, and Asian) do not sum to totals because data are not presented for all races. Persons whose ethnicity is identified as Hispanic or Latino may be of any race.

Source: 2012 Annual Social and Economic Supplement, Current Population Survey, U.S. Bureau of Labor Statistics.

Table 7. **Employment status of women, by presence and age of youngest child, March 1975–March 2012**

(Numbers in thousands)

Year	With children under age 18					With children ages 6 to 17, none younger				
	Civilian labor force		Employed	Unemployed		Civilian labor force		Employed	Unemployed	
	Total	Percentage of population		Total	Percentage of labor force	Total	Percentage of population		Total	Percentage of labor force
1975.......	14,616	47.4	13,069	1,548	11.0	8,917	54.9	8,218	700	7.9
1976.......	15,073	48.8	13,725	1,346	8.9	9,388	56.2	8,769	621	6.6
1977.......	15,669	50.8	14,276	1,393	8.9	10,040	58.3	9,389	650	6.5
1978.......	16,385	53.0	15,142	1,242	7.6	10,401	60.0	9,845	556	5.3
1979.......	16,883	54.5	15,624	1,259	7.7	10,646	61.6	10,030	615	5.8
1980......	17,790	56.6	16,526	1,264	7.1	11,252	64.3	10,640	612	5.4
1981.......	18,422	58.1	16,952	1,471	8.0	11,490	65.5	10,725	765	6.7
1982.......	18,744	58.5	16,854	1,890	10.1	11,377	65.8	10,440	936	8.2
1983.......	18,924	58.9	16,792	2,131	11.3	11,340	66.3	10,303	1,037	9.1
1984......	19,555	60.5	17,782	1,773	9.1	11,538	68.1	10,739	799	6.9
1985......	20,041	62.1	18,306	1,735	8.7	11,826	69.9	10,984	842	7.1
1986......	20,620	62.8	18,922	1,698	8.2	12,075	70.4	11,320	756	6.3
1987......	21,422	64.7	19,798	1,624	7.6	12,438	72.0	11,661	778	6.3
1988......	21,545	65.1	20,141	1,404	6.5	12,683	73.3	12,042	641	5.1
1989......	21,936	65.7	20,647	1,289	5.9	12,800	74.2	12,168	632	4.9
1990.......	22,196	66.7	20,865	1,331	6.0	12,799	74.7	12,133	666	5.2
1991.......	22,327	66.6	20,774	1,552	7.0	12,691	74.4	12,017	674	5.3
1992.......	22,756	67.2	21,052	1,704	7.5	13,183	75.9	12,391	793	6.0
1993......	23,063	66.9	21,521	1,541	6.7	13,441	75.4	12,757	684	5.1
1994......	24,191	68.4	22,467	1,724	7.1	13,863	76.0	13,074	789	5.7
1995......	24,695	69.7	23,195	1,500	6.1	14,300	76.4	13,608	691	4.8
1996......	24,720	70.2	23,386	1,334	5.4	14,427	77.2	13,794	633	4.4
1997......	25,604	72.1	24,082	1,522	5.9	14,993	78.1	14,282	711	4.7
1998......	25,647	72.3	24,209	1,438	5.6	15,028	78.4	14,370	658	4.4
1999......	25,472	72.1	24,307	1,165	4.6	15,150	78.5	14,633	516	3.4
2000......	25,795	72.9	24,693	1,102	4.3	15,479	79.0	14,931	549	3.5
2001.......	26,269	72.7	25,030	1,239	4.7	15,839	79.4	15,220	619	3.9
2002......	26,140	72.2	24,612	1,529	5.8	15,948	78.6	15,171	777	4.9
2003.......	26,202	71.7	24,598	1,603	6.1	15,993	78.7	15,166	828	5.2
2004......	25,913	70.7	24,413	1,501	5.8	15,782	77.5	15,006	776	4.9
2005......	25,941	70.5	24,564	1,377	5.3	15,594	76.9	14,930	663	4.3
2006......	26,009	70.6	24,728	1,281	4.9	15,579	76.9	14,949	630	4.0
2007......	26,834	71.3	25,646	1,188	4.4	15,940	77.7	15,341	599	3.8
2008......	25,930	71.2	24,637	1,294	5.0	15,479	77.5	14,842	636	4.1
2009......	26,122	71.6	24,079	2,043	7.8	15,625	78.2	14,562	1,063	6.8
2010.......	25,783	71.3	23,510	2,273	8.8	15,247	77.2	14,058	1,189	7.8
2011.......	25,376	70.9	23,109	2,266	8.9	14,973	76.5	13,842	1,131	7.6
2012.......	25,384	70.9	23,366	2,018	7.9	14,922	76.0	13,908	1,014	6.8

See note at end of table.

Table 7. **Employment status of women, by presence and age of youngest child, March 1975–March 2012 (continued)**

(Numbers in thousands)

Year	With children under age 6					With children under age 3				
	Civilian labor force		Employed	Unemployed		Civilian labor force		Employed	Unemployed	
	Total	Percentage of population		Total	Percentage of labor force	Total	Percentage of population		Total	Percentage of labor force
1975.......	5,699	39.0	4,851	848	14.9	2,824	34.3	2,326	500	17.7
1976.......	5,684	40.1	4,957	727	12.8	2,702	34.1	2,285	418	15.5
1977.......	5,629	41.2	4,887	742	13.2	2,795	35.4	2,371	424	15.2
1978.......	5,983	44.0	5,297	687	11.5	3,179	39.4	2,768	411	12.9
1979.......	6,238	45.7	5,594	644	10.3	3,380	41.1	2,979	401	11.9
1980.......	6,538	46.8	5,886	652	10.0	3,565	41.9	3,167	398	11.2
1981.......	6,933	48.9	6,227	706	10.2	3,826	44.3	3,380	446	11.7
1982.......	7,367	49.9	6,414	953	12.9	4,133	45.6	3,542	591	14.3
1983.......	7,583	50.5	6,489	1,094	14.4	4,233	46.0	3,551	682	16.1
1984.......	8,017	52.1	7,043	974	12.1	4,401	47.6	3,839	562	12.8
1985.......	8,215	53.5	7,322	893	10.9	4,601	49.5	4,089	513	11.1
1986.......	8,545	54.4	7,602	943	11.0	4,786	50.8	4,227	559	11.7
1987.......	8,983	56.7	8,137	846	9.4	5,064	52.9	4,570	494	9.8
1988.......	8,862	56.1	8,099	763	8.6	4,947	52.4	4,477	470	9.5
1989.......	9,136	56.7	8,478	657	7.2	5,053	52.4	4,671	381	7.5
1990.......	9,397	58.2	8,732	664	7.1	5,216	53.6	4,823	393	7.5
1991.......	9,636	58.4	8,758	878	9.1	5,417	54.5	4,868	550	10.1
1992.......	9,573	58.0	8,662	911	9.5	5,329	54.5	4,776	553	10.4
1993.......	9,621	57.9	8,764	857	8.9	5,349	53.9	4,857	492	9.2
1994.......	10,328	60.3	9,394	935	9.0	5,724	57.1	5,165	559	9.8
1995.......	10,395	62.3	9,587	809	7.8	5,650	58.7	5,172	478	8.5
1996.......	10,293	62.3	9,592	701	6.8	5,619	59.0	5,222	397	7.1
1997.......	10,610	65.0	9,800	810	7.6	5,839	61.8	5,366	473	8.1
1998.......	10,619	65.2	9,839	780	7.3	5,882	62.2	5,454	428	7.3
1999.......	10,322	64.4	9,674	648	6.3	5,645	60.7	5,285	359	6.4
2000.......	10,316	65.3	9,763	553	5.4	5,670	61.0	5,350	320	5.6
2001.......	10,430	64.4	9,810	620	5.9	5,743	60.7	5,350	393	6.8
2002.......	10,193	64.1	9,441	752	7.4	5,600	60.5	5,160	440	7.9
2003.......	10,209	62.9	9,433	776	7.6	5,568	58.7	5,112	456	8.2
2004.......	10,131	62.2	9,407	724	7.1	5,401	57.3	4,983	417	7.7
2005.......	10,347	62.6	9,634	714	6.9	5,704	58.9	5,299	405	7.1
2006.......	10,430	63.0	9,779	651	6.2	5,842	59.9	5,458	384	6.6
2007.......	10,894	63.5	10,305	589	5.4	6,006	60.1	5,679	327	5.5
2008.......	10,452	63.6	9,794	657	6.3	5,754	59.6	5,380	374	6.5
2009.......	10,497	63.6	9,517	980	9.3	5,960	61.1	5,401	559	9.4
2010.......	10,536	64.2	9,452	1,085	10.3	5,878	61.1	5,240	638	10.9
2011.......	10,403	64.2	9,268	1,135	10.9	5,639	60.9	5,006	633	11.2
2012.......	10,462	64.7	9,458	1,004	9.6	5,529	60.7	4,960	569	10.3

See note at end of table.

Table 7. **Employment status of women, by presence and age of youngest child, March 1975–March 2012 (continued)**
(Numbers in thousands)

Year	With no children under age 18				
	Civilian labor force		Employed	Unemployed	
	Total	Percentage of population		Total	Percentage of labor force
1975.......	22,365	45.1	20,381	1,984	8.9
1976.......	23,327	45.7	21,389	1,938	8.3
1977.......	24,385	46.4	22,348	2,037	8.4
1978.......	25,362	47.0	23,631	1,731	6.8
1979.......	26,962	48.6	25,285	1,677	6.2
1980.......	27,144	48.1	25,375	1,769	6.5
1981.......	27,992	48.7	25,934	2,059	7.4
1982.......	28,351	48.6	26,041	2,311	8.2
1983.......	28,856	48.7	26,373	2,483	8.6
1984.......	29,684	49.3	27,652	2,032	6.8
1985.......	30,850	50.4	28,814	2,036	6.6
1986.......	31,112	50.5	29,107	2,005	6.4
1987.......	31,538	50.5	29,688	1,850	5.9
1988.......	32,490	51.2	30,911	1,580	4.9
1989.......	33,255	51.9	31,761	1,495	4.5
1990.......	33,942	52.3	32,391	1,551	4.6
1991.......	34,047	52.0	32,167	1,880	5.5
1992.......	34,487	52.3	32,481	2,006	5.8
1993.......	34,495	52.1	32,476	2,020	5.9
1994.......	35,455	53.1	33,345	2,110	6.0
1995.......	35,843	52.9	34,054	1,789	5.0
1996.......	36,509	53.0	34,698	1,811	5.0
1997.......	37,295	53.6	35,572	1,723	4.6
1998.......	38,253	54.1	36,680	1,573	4.1
1999.......	39,314	54.3	37,587	1,727	4.4
2000.......	40,142	54.8	38,408	1,733	4.3
2001.......	40,996	54.4	39,363	1,633	4.0
2002.......	41,278	54.0	39,038	2,241	5.4
2003.......	42,039	54.1	39,667	2,372	5.6
2004.......	42,289	53.8	40,000	2,289	5.4
2005.......	42,677	53.5	40,570	2,107	4.9
2006.......	43,392	53.6	41,440	1,952	4.5
2007.......	44,039	53.9	42,279	1,760	4.0
2008.......	45,585	54.3	43,417	2,168	4.8
2009.......	45,649	53.8	42,343	3,306	7.2
2010.......	46,098	53.5	42,256	3,842	8.3
2011.......	46,198	53.0	42,569	3,629	7.9
2012.......	47,222	52.6	43,494	3,728	7.9

Note: Children are parents' "own" children and include sons, daughters, stepchildren, or adopted children. Not included are nieces, nephews, grandchildren, and other related and unrelated children. Data for 1994 and subsequent years are not directly comparable with data for 1993 and earlier years because of the introduction of a major redesign of the Current Population Survey.

Source: 1975 to 2012 Annual Social and Economic Supplements, Current Population Survey, U.S. Bureau of Labor Statistics.

Table 8. **Employment status of the civilian noninstitutional population 25 to 64 years of age, by educational attainment and gender, 2012 annual averages**

(Numbers in thousands)

Educational attainment and gender	Civilian noninsti-tutional population	Civilian labor force						Not in labor force
		Total	Percentage of population	Employed		Unemployed		
				Total	Percentage of population	Total	Percentage of labor force	
Total								
Total, 25 to 64 years........................	162,632	125,963	77.5	117,390	72.2	8,573	6.8	36,669
Less than a high school diploma........	17,242	10,566	61.3	9,221	53.5	1,345	12.7	6,676
High school graduates, no college.....	47,004	34,576	73.6	31,656	67.3	2,920	8.4	12,427
Some college or associate's degree...	45,113	35,470	78.6	32,959	73.1	2,511	7.1	9,642
College graduates, total..................	53,273	45,350	85.1	43,554	81.8	1,796	4.0	7,923
Bachelor's degree.........................	34,833	29,313	84.2	28,015	80.4	1,297	4.4	5,520
Master's degree............................	13,635	11,715	85.9	11,314	83.0	401	3.4	1,920
Professional degree......................	2,397	2,131	88.9	2,089	87.1	42	2.0	267
Doctoral degree............................	2,407	2,191	91.0	2,135	88.7	56	2.6	216
Women								
Total, 25 to 64 years........................	83,256	59,031	70.9	55,011	66.1	4,019	6.8	24,226
Less than a high school diploma........	8,117	3,856	47.5	3,298	40.6	558	14.5	4,261
High school graduates, no college.....	22,562	14,732	65.3	13,512	59.9	1,221	8.3	7,829
Some college or associate's degree...	24,358	17,931	73.6	16,633	68.3	1,298	7.2	6,427
College graduates, total..................	28,219	22,511	79.8	21,569	76.4	942	4.2	5,708
Bachelor's degree.........................	18,526	14,493	78.2	13,829	74.6	664	4.6	4,033
Master's degree............................	7,699	6,317	82.1	6,091	79.1	226	3.6	1,381
Professional degree......................	998	828	83.0	803	80.5	24	3.0	170
Doctoral degree............................	997	873	87.6	845	84.8	27	3.1	124
Men								
Total, 25 to 64 years........................	79,376	66,932	84.3	62,379	78.6	4,554	6.8	12,443
Less than a high school diploma........	9,125	6,710	73.5	5,923	64.9	787	11.7	2,415
High school graduates, no college.....	24,442	19,844	81.2	18,144	74.2	1,699	8.6	4,598
Some college or associate's degree...	20,754	17,539	84.5	16,326	78.7	1,213	6.9	3,215
College graduates, total..................	25,054	22,839	91.2	21,985	87.8	854	3.7	2,215
Bachelor's degree.........................	16,307	14,819	90.9	14,186	87.0	633	4.3	1,488
Master's degree............................	5,937	5,398	90.9	5,224	88.0	175	3.2	539
Professional degree......................	1,400	1,303	93.1	1,286	91.9	17	1.3	97
Doctoral degree............................	1,411	1,318	93.5	1,289	91.4	29	2.2	92

Source: Current Population Survey, U.S. Bureau of Labor Statistics.

Table 9. **Percent distribution of the civilian labor force 25 to 64 years of age, by educational attainment and gender, 1970–2012**

Year	Civilian labor force (thousands)	Percent distribution				
		Total	High school		College	
			Less than 4 years	4 years, no college	1 to 3 years	4 years or more
		Total				
1970[1]	61,765	100.0	36.1	38.1	11.8	14.1
1971	62,344	100.0	34.5	38.4	12.3	14.8
1972	63,704	100.0	33.3	38.8	12.4	15.5
1973	64,775	100.0	30.9	39.7	13.0	16.4
1974	66,527	100.0	29.3	39.5	13.7	17.5
1975	67,774	100.0	27.5	39.7	14.4	18.3
1976	69,243	100.0	25.8	39.6	15.2	19.4
1977	71,324	100.0	24.9	39.2	15.7	20.2
1978	73,504	100.0	23.7	39.2	16.5	20.6
1979	75,781	100.0	21.8	39.5	17.3	21.3
1980	78,010	100.0	20.6	39.8	17.6	22.0
1981	80,273	100.0	19.7	40.6	17.7	22.0
1982	81,516	100.0	18.8	40.8	17.3	23.1
1983	83,615	100.0	17.8	39.9	18.1	24.2
1984	86,001	100.0	16.7	40.2	18.4	24.7
1985	88,424	100.0	15.9	40.2	19.0	24.9
1986	90,500	100.0	15.5	40.2	19.5	24.8
1987	92,966	100.0	14.9	40.2	19.7	25.3
1988	94,870	100.0	14.7	39.9	19.7	25.7
1989	97,318	100.0	14.0	39.6	20.0	26.4
1990	99,175	100.0	13.4	39.5	20.7	26.4
1991	100,480	100.0	13.0	39.4	21.1	26.5

Year	Civilian labor force (thousands)	Percent distribution				
		Total	Less than a high school diploma	High school graduates, no college	Some college, no degree, or associate's degree	College graduates
		Total				
1992[2]	103,018	100.0	12.1	35.7	25.6	26.6
1993	104,237	100.0	11.3	35.1	26.6	27.0
1994	105,610	100.0	10.8	33.9	27.7	27.6
1995	107,032	100.0	10.4	33.2	28.1	28.3
1996	108,932	100.0	10.6	32.9	27.8	28.7
1997	110,945	100.0	10.6	32.9	27.5	29.0
1998	111,932	100.0	10.5	32.4	27.4	29.8
1999	113,095	100.0	10.0	31.8	27.6	30.5
2000	115,750	100.0	10.1	31.4	27.8	30.7
2001	116,893	100.0	10.1	30.9	28.0	31.0
2002	118,028	100.0	10.0	30.7	27.7	31.6
2003	119,621	100.0	9.9	30.3	27.6	32.1
2004	120,135	100.0	9.7	30.1	27.7	32.4
2005	121,752	100.0	9.8	29.9	27.8	32.5
2006	123,550	100.0	9.7	29.6	27.7	33.0
2007	125,104	100.0	9.3	29.2	27.7	33.8
2008	126,011	100.0	9.0	28.8	28.0	34.2
2009	126,247	100.0	9.0	28.6	28.0	34.4
2010	126,237	100.0	8.9	28.6	27.9	34.6
2011	125,508	100.0	8.7	28.0	28.0	35.3
2012	125,963	100.0	8.4	27.4	28.2	36.0

See footnotes at end of table.

Table 9. **Percent distribution of the civilian labor force 25 to 64 years of age, by educational attainment and gender, 1970–2012 (continued)**

Year	Civilian labor force (thousands)	Percent distribution				
		Total	High school		College	
			Less than 4 years	4 years, no college	1 to 3 years	4 years or more
Women						
1970[1]...........	22,462	100.0	33.5	44.3	10.9	11.2
1971.............	22,804	100.0	32.2	44.2	11.9	11.8
1972.............	23,606	100.0	30.7	45.1	11.8	12.4
1973.............	24,158	100.0	28.4	45.9	12.4	13.3
1974.............	25,203	100.0	26.7	45.3	13.4	14.6
1975.............	26,146	100.0	26.5	45.5	13.9	14.1
1976.............	27,166	100.0	24.0	45.1	14.7	16.2
1977.............	28,369	100.0	22.8	45.1	15.2	16.9
1978.............	29,738	100.0	22.0	44.9	16.1	17.0
1979.............	31,151	100.0	20.1	45.0	17.1	17.8
1980.............	32,593	100.0	18.4	45.4	17.4	18.7
1981.............	33,910	100.0	17.4	46.1	17.9	18.6
1982.............	34,870	100.0	16.6	45.6	18.3	19.5
1983.............	35,712	100.0	15.6	44.8	18.8	20.9
1984.............	37,234	100.0	14.5	44.9	18.9	21.7
1985.............	38,779	100.0	13.7	44.4	19.9	22.0
1986.............	39,767	100.0	13.2	44.3	20.3	22.2
1987.............	41,105	100.0	12.5	44.0	20.7	22.8
1988.............	42,254	100.0	12.4	43.3	21.2	23.1
1989.............	43,650	100.0	11.9	42.9	20.9	24.3
1990.............	44,699	100.0	11.3	42.4	21.9	24.5
1991.............	45,315	100.0	10.9	41.6	22.2	25.2

Year	Civilian labor force (thousands)	Percent distribution				
		Total	Less than a high school diploma	High school graduates, no college	Some college, no degree, or associate's degree	College graduates
Women						
1992[2]...........	46,589	100.0	10.3	37.4	27.3	25.0
1993.............	47,245	100.0	9.3	36.6	28.4	25.7
1994.............	48,405	100.0	9.0	35.0	29.8	26.2
1995.............	49,247	100.0	8.8	34.1	30.2	26.9
1996.............	50,240	100.0	8.8	33.6	29.9	27.8
1997.............	51,261	100.0	8.7	33.5	29.4	28.4
1998.............	51,678	100.0	8.8	32.7	29.4	29.2
1999.............	52,525	100.0	8.5	32.1	29.5	29.9
2000.............	53,749	100.0	8.5	31.6	29.8	30.1
2001.............	54,229	100.0	8.4	31.0	30.2	30.4
2002.............	54,710	100.0	8.1	30.6	29.9	31.3
2003.............	55,596	100.0	7.9	30.0	29.9	32.2
2004.............	55,616	100.0	7.7	29.4	30.2	32.6
2005.............	56,322	100.0	7.7	28.7	30.2	33.3
2006.............	57,201	100.0	7.6	28.3	30.2	33.9
2007.............	57,791	100.0	7.1	27.9	30.1	34.9
2008.............	58,465	100.0	6.9	27.2	30.4	35.6
2009.............	58,787	100.0	7.0	26.7	30.3	36.0
2010.............	58,808	100.0	6.8	26.4	30.3	36.4
2011.............	58,520	100.0	6.7	25.8	30.4	37.1
2012.............	59,031	100.0	6.5	25.0	30.4	38.1

See footnotes at end of table.

BLS Reports | May 2014 • www.bls.gov

Table 9. **Percent distribution of the civilian labor force 25 to 64 years of age, by educational attainment and gender, 1970–2012 (continued)**

Year	Civilian labor force (thousands)	Percent distribution				
		Total	High school		College	
			Less than 4 years	4 years, no college	1 to 3 years	4 years or more
		Men				
1970[1]............	39,303	100.0	37.5	34.5	12.2	15.7
1971............	39,539	100.0	35.9	35.1	12.5	16.5
1972............	40,098	100.0	34.8	35.1	12.8	17.3
1973............	40,617	100.0	32.4	36.0	13.4	18.2
1974............	41,344	100.0	30.8	36.0	13.9	19.3
1975............	41,628	100.0	28.9	36.1	14.8	20.2
1976............	42,077	100.0	27.0	36.0	15.5	21.5
1977............	42,954	100.0	26.3	35.3	16.1	22.3
1978............	43,766	100.0	24.8	35.3	16.9	23.0
1979............	44,630	100.0	23.0	35.7	17.5	23.8
1980............	45,417	100.0	22.2	35.7	17.7	24.3
1981............	46,363	100.0	21.5	36.5	17.4	24.6
1982............	47,144	100.0	20.3	36.8	17.5	25.5
1983............	47,903	100.0	19.4	36.3	17.7	26.6
1984............	48,767	100.0	18.4	36.7	18.0	26.9
1985............	49,647	100.0	17.7	36.9	18.3	27.1
1986............	50,733	100.0	17.2	37.0	18.9	26.9
1987............	51,860	100.0	16.8	37.1	18.9	27.2
1988............	52,616	100.0	16.5	37.3	18.5	27.8
1989............	53,668	100.0	15.7	36.9	19.2	28.2
1990............	54,476	100.0	15.1	37.2	19.7	28.0
1991............	55,165	100.0	14.7	37.5	20.2	27.6

See footnotes at end of table.

Table 9. **Percent distribution of the civilian labor force 25 to 64 years of age, by educational attainment and gender, 1970–2012 (continued)**

Year	Civilian labor force (thousands)	Percent distribution				
		Total	Less than a high school diploma	High school graduates, no college	Some college, no degree, or associate's degree	College graduates
			Men			
1992[2]............	56,428	100.0	13.7	34.2	24.3	27.8
1993.............	56,992	100.0	12.9	33.9	25.1	28.1
1994.............	57,205	100.0	12.4	33.0	25.9	28.8
1995.............	57,784	100.0	11.8	32.4	26.3	29.4
1996.............	58,692	100.0	12.2	32.3	26.1	29.4
1997.............	59,684	100.0	12.2	32.4	25.9	29.6
1998.............	60,255	100.0	12.0	32.1	25.6	30.3
1999.............	60,570	100.0	11.4	31.6	26.0	31.0
2000.............	62,001	100.0	11.5	31.2	26.1	31.2
2001.............	62,664	100.0	11.5	30.9	26.2	31.4
2002.............	63,318	100.0	11.6	30.8	25.8	31.8
2003.............	64,025	100.0	11.7	30.6	25.6	32.1
2004.............	64,519	100.0	11.5	30.7	25.6	32.3
2005.............	65,430	100.0	11.5	30.9	25.7	31.9
2006.............	66,350	100.0	11.5	30.6	25.5	32.3
2007.............	67,313	100.0	11.2	30.4	25.6	32.9
2008.............	67,546	100.0	10.9	30.2	25.9	33.0
2009.............	67,460	100.0	10.8	30.3	25.9	33.0
2010.............	67,429	100.0	10.6	30.6	25.8	33.0
2011.............	66,989	100.0	10.4	30.0	26.0	33.7
2012.............	66,932	100.0	10.0	29.6	26.2	34.1

[1] Data from 1970 to 1991 are from the March Current Population Survey. The educational attainment categories for these years were based on the number of years of school completed.

[2] Data beginning in 1992 are annual averages, and the educational attainment categories are based on the highest diploma or degree received.

Source: Current Population Survey, U.S. Bureau of Labor Statistics.

Table 10. **Employed persons, by major occupation and gender, 2011 and 2012 annual averages**

(Numbers in thousands)

Occupation and gender	Year			
	2011		2012	
	Number	Percent	Number	Percent
Total				
Total, 16 years and older.............................	139,869	100.0	142,469	100.0
Management, professional, and related occupations	52,547	37.6	54,043	37.9
Management, business, and financial operations occupations	21,589	15.4	22,678	15.9
Professional and related occupations	30,957	22.1	31,365	22.0
Service occupations	24,787	17.7	25,459	17.9
Sales and office occupations	33,066	23.6	33,152	23.3
Sales and related occupations	15,330	11.0	15,457	10.8
Office and administrative support occupations	17,736	12.7	17,695	12.4
Natural resources, construction, and maintenance occupations	13,009	9.3	12,821	9.0
Farming, fishing, and forestry occupations	1,001	.7	994	.7
Construction and extraction occupations	7,125	5.1	7,005	4.9
Installation, maintenance, and repair occupations	4,883	3.5	4,821	3.4
Production, transportation, and material moving occupations	16,461	11.8	16,994	11.9
Production occupations	8,142	5.8	8,455	5.9
Transportation and material moving occupations	8,318	5.9	8,540	6.0
Women				
Total, 16 years and older..............................	65,579	100.0	66,914	100.0
Management, professional, and related occupations	26,995	41.2	27,834	41.6
Management, business, and financial operations occupations	9,314	14.2	9,899	14.8
Professional and related occupations	17,681	27.0	17,936	26.8
Service occupations	13,858	21.1	14,324	21.4
Sales and office occupations	20,616	31.4	20,500	30.6
Sales and related occupations	7,597	11.6	7,535	11.3
Office and administrative support occupations	13,019	19.9	12,965	19.4
Natural resources, construction, and maintenance occupations	552	.8	554	.8
Farming, fishing, and forestry occupations	216	.3	226	.3
Construction and extraction occupations	163	.2	173	.3
Installation, maintenance, and repair occupations	173	.3	156	.2
Production, transportation, and material moving occupations	3,558	5.4	3,701	5.5
Production occupations	2,316	3.5	2,346	3.5
Transportation and material moving occupations	1,242	1.9	1,355	2.0

See note at end of table.

Table 10. **Employed persons, by major occupation and gender, 2011 and 2012 annual averages (continued)**

(Numbers in thousands)

Occupation and gender	Year			
	2011		2012	
	Number	Percent	Number	Percent
Men				
Total, 16 years and older..	74,290	100.0	75,555	100.0
Management, professional, and related occupations	25,552	34.4	26,208	34.7
Management, business, and financial operations occupations	12,275	16.5	12,779	16.9
Professional and related occupations	13,277	17.9	13,429	17.8
Service occupations	10,929	14.7	11,135	14.7
Sales and office occupations	12,450	16.8	12,653	16.7
Sales and related occupations	7,733	10.4	7,922	10.5
Office and administrative support occupations	4,717	6.3	4,730	6.3
Natural resources, construction, and maintenance occupations	12,457	16.8	12,266	16.2
Farming, fishing, and forestry occupations	785	1.1	768	1.0
Construction and extraction occupations	6,962	9.4	6,832	9.0
Installation, maintenance, and repair occupations	4,710	6.3	4,666	6.2
Production, transportation, and material moving occupations	12,902	17.4	13,294	17.6
Production occupations	5,826	7.8	6,109	8.1
Transportation and material moving occupations	7,076	9.5	7,185	9.5

Source: Current Population Survey, U.S. Bureau of Labor Statistics.

Table 11. **Employed persons, by detailed occupation and gender, 2012 annual averages**

(Numbers in thousands)

Occupation	Total employed	Percent women
Total, 16 years and older..	142,469	47.0
Management, professional, and related occupations.............................	54,043	51.5
Management, business, and financial operations occupations...................	22,678	43.6
Management occupations..	16,042	38.6
Chief executives..	1,513	27.4
General and operations managers....................................	1,064	29.1
Legislators...	11	–
Advertising and promotions managers................................	77	49.4
Marketing and sales managers......................................	967	45.2
Public relations and fundraising managers.............................	58	69.3
Administrative services managers....................................	144	44.1
Computer and information systems managers...........................	605	26.8
Financial managers..	1,228	53.5
Compensation and benefits managers.................................	15	–
Human resources managers..	224	72.7
Training and development managers..................................	36	–
Industrial production managers.....................................	261	17.6
Purchasing managers..	218	50.9
Transportation, storage, and distribution managers.....................	287	15.6
Farmers, ranchers, and other agricultural managers.....................	944	24.5
Construction managers...	983	6.4
Education administrators..	811	64.4
Architectural and engineering managers...............................	120	10.9
Food service managers...	1,085	47.2
Funeral service managers...	13	–
Gaming managers...	26	–
Lodging managers...	154	45.0
Medical and health services managers................................	585	69.7
Natural sciences managers..	18	–
Postmasters and mail superintendents................................	39	–
Property, real estate, and community association managers...............	644	50.7
Social and community service managers...............................	315	70.5
Emergency management directors...................................	6	–
Managers, all other..	3,594	35.0
Business and financial operations occupations............................	6,636	55.8
Agents and business managers of artists, performers, and athletes..........	47	–
Buyers and purchasing agents, farm products..........................	13	–
Wholesale and retail buyers, except farm products......................	198	55.2
Purchasing agents, except wholesale, retail, and farm products............	261	55.1
Claims adjusters, appraisers, examiners, and investigators................	323	63.4
Compliance officers..	199	50.6
Cost estimators...	114	11.7
Human resources workers...	603	71.8
Compensation, benefits, and job analysis specialists....................	71	81.1
Training and development specialists.................................	126	56.4
Logisticians..	94	36.8
Management analysts...	773	39.8
Meeting, convention, and event planners..............................	127	73.3
Fundraisers..	86	75.3
Market research analysts and marketing specialists.....................	219	54.2

See note at end of table.

Table 11. **Employed persons, by detailed occupation and gender, 2012 annual averages (continued)**

(Numbers in thousands)

Occupation	Total employed	Percent women
Business operations specialists, all other.	251	67.3
Accountants and auditors.	1,765	60.9
Appraisers and assessors of real estate.	93	40.6
Budget analysts.	55	52.5
Credit analysts.	30	–
Financial analysts.	89	36.8
Personal financial advisors.	378	31.2
Insurance underwriters.	103	70.4
Financial examiners.	14	–
Credit counselors and loan officers.	333	59.2
Tax examiners and collectors, and revenue agents	82	62.4
Tax preparers.	107	59.6
Financial specialists, all other.	82	66.5
Professional and related occupations.	31,365	57.2
Computer and mathematical occupations.	3,816	25.6
Computer and information research scientists	29	–
Computer systems analysts.	499	30.9
Information security analysts.	52	15.1
Computer programmers.	480	22.5
Software developers, applications and systems software.	1,084	19.7
Web developers.	190	33.7
Computer support specialists.	476	27.1
Database administrators.	101	36.6
Network and computer systems administrators.	226	25.0
Computer network architects.	127	8.1
Computer occupations, all other.	341	24.4
Actuaries.	26	–
Mathematicians.	4	–
Operations research analysts.	130	54.9
Statisticians.	47	–
Miscellaneous mathematical science occupations	3	–
Architecture and engineering occupations.	2,846	13.7
Architects, except naval.	195	23.5
Surveyors, cartographers, and photogrammetrists.	51	27.8
Aerospace engineers.	119	9.0
Agricultural engineers.	4	–
Biomedical engineers.	10	–
Chemical engineers.	71	17.7
Civil engineers.	358	13.7
Computer hardware engineers.	91	15.1
Electrical and electronics engineers.	335	9.0
Environmental engineers.	43	–
Industrial engineers, including health and safety.	197	18.8
Marine engineers and naval architects.	8	–
Materials engineers.	40	–
Mechanical engineers.	288	4.5
Mining and geological engineers, including mining safety engineers	9	–
Nuclear engineers.	11	–
Petroleum engineers.	38	–
Engineers, all other.	359	13.2
Drafters.	149	16.6

See note at end of table.

Table 11. **Employed persons, by detailed occupation and gender, 2012 annual averages (continued)**

(Numbers in thousands)

Occupation	Total employed	Percent women
Engineering technicians, except drafters.	395	16.3
Surveying and mapping technicians.	77	4.3
Life, physical, and social science occupations.	1,316	45.3
Agricultural and food scientists.	42	–
Biological scientists.	101	50.1
Conservation scientists and foresters	25	–
Medical scientists.	136	52.8
Life scientists, all other.	0	–
Astronomers and physicists.	25	–
Atmospheric and space scientists.	15	–
Chemists and materials scientists.	105	44.2
Environmental scientists and geoscientists.	105	25.7
Physical scientists, all other.	154	35.1
Economists.	26	–
Survey researchers.	2	–
Psychologists.	178	72.7
Sociologists.	7	–
Urban and regional planners.	28	–
Miscellaneous social scientists and related workers.	57	54.3
Agricultural and food science technicians.	32	–
Biological technicians.	19	–
Chemical technicians.	70	29.9
Geological and petroleum technicians.	21	–
Nuclear technicians.	3	–
Social science research assistants.	3	–
Miscellaneous life, physical, and social science technicians.	160	52.8
Community and social service occupations.	2,265	63.8
Counselors.	661	69.3
Social workers.	734	80.6
Probation officers and correctional treatment specialists.	88	47.5
Social and human service assistants.	151	77.1
Miscellaneous community and social service specialists, including health educators and community health workers.	94	75.7
Clergy.	408	20.5
Directors, religious activities and education.	61	66.3
Religious workers, all other.	69	62.4
Legal occupations.	1,786	50.4
Lawyers.	1,061	31.1
Judicial law clerks.	17	–
Judges, magistrates, and other judicial workers.	67	39.0
Paralegals and legal assistants.	418	85.9
Miscellaneous legal support workers.	223	79.0
Education, training, and library occupations.	8,543	73.6
Postsecondary teachers.	1,350	48.2
Preschool and kindergarten teachers.	678	98.1
Elementary and middle school teachers.	2,838	81.4
Secondary school teachers.	1,127	57.3
Special education teachers.	366	86.2
Other teachers and instructors.	860	65.6
Archivists, curators, and museum technicians.	46	–
Librarians.	181	86.8

See note at end of table.

Table 11. Employed persons, by detailed occupation and gender, 2012 annual averages (continued)

(Numbers in thousands)

Occupation	Total employed	Percent women
Library technicians.	45	–
Teacher assistants.	898	91.1
Other education, training, and l brary workers.	153	67.3
Arts, design, entertainment, sports, and media occupations.	2,814	48.3
Artists and related workers.	212	51.6
Designers.	756	55.3
Actors.	37	–
Producers and directors.	121	40.8
Athletes, coaches, umpires, and related workers.	267	36.5
Dancers and choreographers.	21	–
Musicians, singers, and related workers.	203	35.5
Entertainers and performers, sports and related workers, all other.	41	–
Announcers.	50	23.6
News analysts, reporters and correspondents.	82	45.7
Public relations specialists.	155	58.2
Editors.	159	50.7
Technical writers.	58	55.5
Writers and authors.	208	55.6
Miscellaneous media and communication workers.	98	79.2
Broadcast and sound engineering technicians and radio operators.	108	8.4
Photographers.	178	52.2
Television, video, and motion picture camera operators and editors.	57	21.4
Media and communication equipment workers, all other.	2	–
Healthcare practitioners and technical occupations.	7,977	75.0
Chiropractors.	58	22.3
Dentists.	167	24.2
Dietitians and nutritionists.	116	93.3
Optometrists.	33	–
Pharmacists.	286	53.7
Physicians and surgeons.	911	34.3
Physician assistants.	108	69.4
Podiatrists.	9	–
Audiologists.	14	–
Occupational therapists.	118	94.0
Physical therapists.	211	70.7
Radiation therapists.	14	–
Recreational therapists.	13	–
Respiratory therapists.	111	60.4
Speech-language pathologists.	146	95.2
Exercise physiologists.	2	–
Therapists, all other.	148	83.6
Veterinarians.	85	54.7
Registered nurses.	2,875	90.6
Nurse anesthetists.	27	–
Nurse midwives.	3	–
Nurse practitioners.	103	86.1
Health diagnosing and treating practitioners, all other.	23	–
Clinical laboratory technologists and technicians.	319	72.8
Dental hygienists.	163	99.3
Diagnostic related technologists and technicians.	308	74.5
Emergency medical technicians and paramedics.	172	31.2

See note at end of table.

Table 11. Employed persons, by detailed occupation and gender, 2012 annual averages (continued)

(Numbers in thousands)

Occupation	Total employed	Percent women
Health practitioner support technologists and technicians.	544	83.6
Licensed practical and licensed vocational nurses.	531	94.2
Medical records and health information technicians.	90	89.3
Opticians, dispensing.	54	59.6
Miscellaneous health technologists and technicians.	140	60.2
Other healthcare practitioners and technical occupations.	75	50.3
Service occupations.	25,459	56.3
Healthcare support occupations.	3,496	87.6
Nursing, psychiatric, and home health aides.	2,119	87.9
Occupational therapy assistants and aides.	18	–
Physical therapist assistants and aides.	66	66.4
Massage therapists.	158	81.5
Dental assistants.	274	97.9
Medical assistants.	429	93.8
Medical transcriptionists.	55	98.2
Pharmacy aides.	45	–
Veterinary assistants and laboratory animal caretakers.	47	–
Phlebotomists.	119	80.2
Miscellaneous healthcare support occupations, including medical equipment preparers.	166	69.0
Protective service occupations.	3,096	20.9
First-line supervisors of correctional officers.	46	–
First-line supervisors of police and detectives.	112	15.2
First-line supervisors of fire fighting and prevention workers.	64	.5
First-line supervisors of protective service workers, all other.	93	29.9
Firefighters.	295	3.4
Fire inspectors.	18	–
Bailiffs, correctional officers, and jailers.	371	28.0
Detectives and criminal investigators.	160	24.8
Fish and game wardens.	7	–
Parking enforcement workers.	4	–
Police and sheriff's patrol officers.	657	12.6
Transit and railroad police.	3	–
Animal control workers.	11	–
Private detectives and investigators.	103	44.0
Security guards and gaming surveillance officers.	903	18.5
Crossing guards.	61	55.3
Transportation security screeners.	25	–
Lifeguards and other recreational, and all other protective service workers.	162	52.6
Food preparation and serving related occupations.	8,018	54.5
Chefs and head cooks.	403	21.5
First-line supervisors of food preparation and serving workers.	552	59.3
Cooks.	1,970	37.7
Food preparation workers.	868	58.0
Bartenders.	412	59.9
Combined food preparation and serving workers, including fast food.	343	64.9
Counter attendants, cafeteria, food concession, and coffee shop.	233	70.8
Waiters and waitresses.	2,124	71.2
Food servers, nonrestaurant.	217	64.9
Dining room and cafeteria attendants and bartender helpers.	359	43.4
Dishwashers.	271	18.7
Hosts and hostesses, restaurant, lounge, and coffee shop.	260	81.5

See note at end of table.

Table 11. **Employed persons, by detailed occupation and gender, 2012 annual averages (continued)**

(Numbers in thousands)

Occupation	Total employed	Percent women
Food preparation and serving related workers, all other.	6	–
Building and grounds cleaning and maintenance occupations.	5,591	38.6
First-line supervisors of housekeeping and janitorial workers.	277	47.1
First-line supervisors of landscaping, lawn service, and groundskeeping workers	281	7.6
Janitors and building cleaners.	2,205	29.7
Maids and housekeeping cleaners.	1,457	88.1
Pest control workers.	73	4.7
Grounds maintenance workers.	1,298	5.1
Personal care and service occupations.	5,258	77.7
First-line supervisors of gaming workers.	146	43.0
First-line supervisors of personal service workers.	246	70.3
Animal trainers.	44	–
Nonfarm animal caretakers.	179	74.2
Gaming services workers.	106	51.0
Motion picture projectionists.	2	–
Ushers, lobby attendants, and ticket takers.	43	–
Miscellaneous entertainment attendants and related workers.	180	45.4
Embalmers and funeral attendants.	16	–
Morticians, undertakers, and funeral directors.	38	–
Barbers.	109	21.9
Hairdressers, hairstylists, and cosmetologists.	785	92.8
Miscellaneous personal appearance workers.	300	81.5
Baggage porters, bellhops, and concierges.	68	25.0
Tour and travel guides.	51	36.9
Childcare workers.	1,314	94.1
Personal care aides.	1,071	84.7
Recreation and fitness workers.	406	66.5
Residential advisors.	58	61.4
Personal care and service workers, all other.	95	45.7
Sales and office occupations.	33,152	61.8
Sales and related occupations.	15,457	48.7
First-line supervisors of retail sales workers.	3,237	43.4
First-line supervisors of non-retail sales workers.	1,151	24.7
Cashiers.	3,275	71.8
Counter and rental clerks.	139	53.4
Parts salespersons.	106	13.3
Retail salespersons.	3,341	50.2
Advertising sales agents.	230	47.4
Insurance sales agents.	540	44.1
Securities, commodities, and financial services sales agents.	280	27.9
Travel agents.	73	79.0
Sales representatives, services, all other.	457	31.0
Sales representatives, wholesale and manufacturing.	1,277	27.0
Models, demonstrators, and product promoters.	65	83.4
Real estate brokers and sales agents.	761	57.1
Sales engineers.	27	–
Telemarketers.	97	50.3
Door-to-door sales workers, news and street vendors, and related workers	198	62.2
Sales and related workers, all other.	204	47.9
Office and administrative support occupations.	17,695	73.3

See note at end of table.

Table 11. **Employed persons, by detailed occupation and gender, 2012 annual averages (continued)**

(Numbers in thousands)

Occupation	Total employed	Percent women
First-line supervisors of office and administrative support workers.	1,416	68.5
Switchboard operators, including answering service.	35	–
Telephone operators.	42	–
Communications equipment operators, all other.	9	–
Bill and account collectors.	206	69.1
Billing and posting clerks.	475	90.1
Bookkeeping, accounting, and auditing clerks.	1,268	89.1
Gaming cage workers.	8	–
Payroll and timekeeping clerks.	155	92.6
Procurement clerks.	27	–
Tellers.	380	87.3
Financial clerks, all other.	52	68.4
Brokerage clerks.	5	–
Correspondence clerks.	6	–
Court, municipal, and license clerks.	85	77.2
Credit authorizers, checkers, and clerks.	43	–
Customer service representatives.	1,956	67.8
Eligibility interviewers, government programs.	92	81.4
File clerks.	292	81.3
Hotel, motel, and resort desk clerks.	110	64.6
Interviewers, except eligibility and loan.	135	83.7
Library assistants, clerical.	97	84.0
Loan interviewers and clerks.	144	81.2
New accounts clerks.	26	–
Order clerks.	104	58.2
Human resources assistants, except payroll and timekeeping.	132	82.7
Receptionists and information clerks.	1,237	91.5
Reservation and transportation ticket agents and travel clerks.	117	58.6
Information and record clerks, all other.	104	80.2
Cargo and freight agents.	25	–
Couriers and messengers.	213	15.5
Dispatchers.	277	61.5
Meter readers, utilities.	29	–
Postal service clerks.	148	50.0
Postal service mail carriers.	318	37.7
Postal service mail sorters, processors, and processing machine operators.	66	47.6
Production, planning, and expediting clerks.	272	55.0
Shipping, receiving, and traffic clerks.	527	27.8
Stock clerks and order fillers.	1,453	35.5
Weighers, measurers, checkers, and samplers, recordkeeping.	74	49.1
Secretaries and administrative assistants.	2,904	95.3
Computer operators.	102	50.7
Data entry keyers.	337	77.0
Word processors and typists.	119	88.7
Desktop publishers.	3	–
Insurance claims and policy processing clerks.	230	81.9
Mail clerks and mail machine operators, except postal service.	81	41.2
Office clerks, general.	1,103	83.4
Office machine operators, except computer.	46	–
Proofreaders and copy markers.	10	–
Statistical assistants.	32	–

See note at end of table.

Table 11. Employed persons, by detailed occupation and gender, 2012 annual averages (continued)

(Numbers in thousands)

Occupation	Total employed	Percent women
Office and administrative support workers, all other.	570	77.3
Natural resources, construction, and maintenance occupations.	12,821	4.3
Farming, fishing, and forestry occupations.	994	22.7
First-line supervisors of farming, fishing, and forestry workers.	50	14.1
Agricultural inspectors.	16	–
Animal breeders.	6	–
Graders and sorters, agricultural products.	118	59.8
Miscellaneous agricultural workers.	711	18.9
Fishers and related fishing workers.	33	–
Hunters and trappers.	2	–
Forest and conservation workers.	9	–
Logging workers.	49	–
Construction and extraction occupations.	7,005	2.5
First-line supervisors of construction trades and extraction workers.	634	2.8
Boilermakers.	23	–
Brickmasons, blockmasons, and stonemasons.	122	.1
Carpenters.	1,223	1.6
Carpet, floor, and tile installers and finishers.	150	2.2
Cement masons, concrete finishers, and terrazzo workers.	68	2.7
Construction laborers.	1,387	2.9
Paving, surfacing, and tamping equipment operators.	23	–
Pile-driver operators.	4	–
Operating engineers and other construction equipment operators.	348	1.3
Drywall installers, ceiling tile installers, and tapers.	129	.3
Electricians.	692	1.8
Glaziers.	46	–
Insulation workers.	44	–
Painters, construction and maintenance.	485	5.5
Paperhangers.	7	–
Pipelayers, plumbers, pipefitters, and steamfitters.	534	1.3
Plasterers and stucco masons.	18	–
Reinforcing iron and rebar workers.	8	–
Roofers.	196	1.5
Sheet metal workers.	123	4.6
Structural iron and steel workers.	65	2.8
Solar photovoltaic installers.	7	–
Helpers—construction trades.	53	4.5
Construction and building inspectors.	118	7.8
Elevator installers and repairers.	29	–
Fence erectors.	33	–
Hazardous materials removal workers.	38	–
Highway maintenance workers.	108	1.5
Rail-track laying and maintenance equipment operators.	10	–
Septic tank servicers and sewer pipe cleaners.	8	–
Miscellaneous construction and related workers.	32	–
Derrick, rotary drill, and service unit operators, oil, gas, and mining.	37	–
Earth drillers, except oil and gas.	35	–
Explosives workers, ordnance handling experts, and blasters.	8	–
Mining machine operators.	65	.3
Roof bolters, mining.	3	–
Roustabouts, oil and gas.	14	–

See note at end of table.

Table 11. **Employed persons, by detailed occupation and gender, 2012 annual averages (continued)**

(Numbers in thousands)

Occupation	Total employed	Percent women
Helpers—extraction workers.	5	–
Other extraction workers.	75	4.5
Installation, maintenance, and repair occupations.	4,821	3.2
First-line supervisors of mechanics, installers, and repairers.	292	5.9
Computer, automated teller, and office machine repairers.	296	10.7
Radio and telecommunications equipment installers and repairers.	158	5.8
Avionics technicians.	14	–
Electric motor, power tool, and related repairers.	37	–
Electrical and electronics installers and repairers, transportation equipment.	5	–
Electrical and electronics repairers, industrial and utility.	12	–
Electronic equipment installers and repairers, motor vehicles.	18	–
Electronic home entertainment equipment installers and repairers.	50	.5
Security and fire alarm systems installers.	41	–
Aircraft mechanics and service technicians.	153	1.6
Automotive body and related repairers.	140	1.8
Automotive glass installers and repairers.	22	–
Automotive service technicians and mechanics.	867	1.2
Bus and truck mechanics and diesel engine specialists.	316	.5
Heavy vehicle and mobile equipment service technicians and mechanics.	194	1.0
Small engine mechanics.	56	1.4
Miscellaneous vehicle and mobile equipment mechanics, installers, and repairers	87	1.8
Control and valve installers and repairers.	27	–
Heating, air conditioning, and refrigeration mechanics and installers.	340	1.6
Home appliance repairers.	47	–
Industrial and refractory machinery mechanics.	454	1.9
Maintenance and repair workers, general.	442	2.2
Maintenance workers, machinery.	28	–
Millwrights.	53	6.4
Electrical power-line installers and repairers.	110	2.4
Telecommunications line installers and repairers.	177	4.8
Precision instrument and equipment repairers.	60	16.0
Wind turbine service technicians.	3	–
Coin, vending, and amusement machine servicers and repairers.	33	–
Commercial divers.	3	–
Locksmiths and safe repairers.	31	–
Manufactured building and mobile home installers.	5	–
Riggers.	13	–
Signal and track switch repairers.	5	–
Helpers—installation, maintenance, and repair workers.	30	–
Other installation, maintenance, and repair workers.	205	3.6
Production, transportation, and material moving occupations.	16,994	21.8
Production occupations.	8,455	27.7
First-line supervisors of production and operating workers.	808	19.5
Aircraft structure, surfaces, rigging, and systems assemblers.	23	–
Electrical, electronics, and electromechanical assemblers.	166	52.8
Engine and other machine assemblers.	32	–
Structural metal fabricators and fitters.	25	–
Miscellaneous assemblers and fabricators.	919	38.4
Bakers.	199	53.9
Butchers and other meat, poultry, and fish processing workers.	311	23.0

See note at end of table.

Table 11. **Employed persons, by detailed occupation and gender, 2012 annual averages (continued)**

(Numbers in thousands)

Occupation	Total employed	Percent women
Food and tobacco roasting, baking, and drying machine operators and tenders.	11	–
Food batchmakers.	84	59.6
Food cooking machine operators and tenders.	14	–
Food processing workers, all other.	117	29.5
Computer control programmers and operators.	67	8.4
Extruding and drawing machine setters, operators, and tenders, metal and plastic.	10	–
Forging machine setters, operators, and tenders, metal and plastic.	10	–
Rolling machine setters, operators, and tenders, metal and plastic.	8	–
Cutting, punching, and press machine setters, operators, and tenders, metal and plastic.	87	18.9
Drilling and boring machine tool setters, operators, and tenders, metal and plastic.	3	–
Grinding, lapping, polishing, and buffing machine tool setters, operators, and tenders, metal and plastic.	54	6.6
Lathe and turning machine tool setters, operators, and tenders, metal and plastic.	17	–
Milling and planing machine setters, operators, and tenders, metal and plastic.	3	–
Machinists.	397	3.8
Metal furnace operators, tenders, pourers, and casters.	17	–
Model makers and patternmakers, metal and plastic.	11	–
Molders and molding machine setters, operators, and tenders, metal and plastic.	37	–
Multiple machine tool setters, operators, and tenders, metal and plastic.	5	–
Tool and die makers.	56	.8
Welding, soldering, and brazing workers.	593	4.8
Heat treating equipment setters, operators, and tenders, metal and plastic.	4	–
Layout workers, metal and plastic.	4	–
Plating and coating machine setters, operators, and tenders, metal and plastic.	18	–
Tool grinders, filers, and sharpeners.	3	–
Metal workers and plastic workers, all other.	375	19.5
Prepress technicians and workers.	33	–
Printing press operators.	201	17.2
Print binding and finishing workers.	22	–
Laundry and dry-cleaning workers.	185	53.3
Pressers, textile, garment, and related materials.	54	70.6
Sewing machine operators.	166	74.2
Shoe and leather workers and repairers.	11	–
Shoe machine operators and tenders.	11	–
Tailors, dressmakers, and sewers.	86	77.1
Textile bleaching and dyeing machine operators and tenders.	5	–
Textile cutting machine setters, operators, and tenders.	12	–
Textile knitting and weaving machine setters, operators, and tenders.	7	–
Textile winding, twisting, and drawing out machine setters, operators, and tenders	14	–
Extruding and forming machine setters, operators, and tenders, synthetic and glass fibers.	1	–
Fabric and apparel patternmakers.	3	–
Upholsterers.	34	–
Textile, apparel, and furnishings workers, all other.	14	–
Cabinetmakers and bench carpenters.	45	–
Furniture finishers.	7	–
Model makers and patternmakers, wood.	0	–
Sawing machine setters, operators, and tenders, wood.	30	–
Woodworking machine setters, operators, and tenders, except sawing.	21	–
Woodworkers, all other.	21	–
Power plant operators, distributors, and dispatchers.	44	–
Stationary engineers and boiler operators.	121	5.5

See note at end of table.

Table 11. **Employed persons, by detailed occupation and gender, 2012 annual averages (continued)**

(Numbers in thousands)

Occupation	Total employed	Percent women
Water and wastewater treatment plant and system operators.	72	4.5
Miscellaneous plant and system operators.	39	–
Chemical processing machine setters, operators, and tenders.	68	16.2
Crushing, grinding, polishing, mixing, and blending workers.	100	15.0
Cutting workers.	67	19.2
Extruding, forming, pressing, and compacting machine setters, operators, and tenders.	45	–
Furnace, kiln, oven, drier, and kettle operators and tenders.	16	–
Inspectors, testers, sorters, samplers, and weighers.	689	33.4
Jewelers and precious stone and metal workers.	46	–
Medical, dental, and ophthalmic laboratory technicians.	95	50.7
Packaging and filling machine operators and tenders.	261	52.3
Painting workers.	150	15.1
Photographic process workers and processing machine operators.	55	45.6
Semiconductor processors.	4	–
Adhesive bonding machine operators and tenders.	9	–
Cleaning, washing, and metal pickling equipment operators and tenders.	7	–
Cooling and freezing equipment operators and tenders.	2	–
Etchers and engravers.	6	–
Molders, shapers, and casters, except metal and plastic.	41	–
Paper goods machine setters, operators, and tenders.	35	–
Tire builders.	19	–
Helpers—production workers.	59	34.8
Production workers, all other.	933	26.3
Transportation and material moving occupations.	8,540	15.9
Supervisors of transportation and material moving workers.	200	23.0
Aircraft pilots and flight engineers.	129	4.1
Air traffic controllers and airfield operations specialists.	44	–
Flight attendants.	88	77.6
Ambulance drivers and attendants, except emergency medical technicians.	20	–
Bus drivers.	558	45.5
Driver/sales workers and truck drivers.	3,201	5.4
Taxi drivers and chauffeurs.	336	13.2
Motor vehicle operators, all other.	63	13.3
Locomotive engineers and operators.	41	–
Railroad brake, signal, and switch operators.	10	–
Railroad conductors and yardmasters.	52	5.6
Subway, streetcar, and other rail transportation workers.	11	–
Sailors and marine oilers.	16	–
Ship and boat captains and operators.	37	–
Ship engineers.	7	–
Bridge and lock tenders.	7	–
Parking lot attendants.	81	11.6
Automotive and watercraft service attendants.	94	9.2
Transportation inspectors.	36	–
Transportation attendants, except flight attendants.	38	–
Other transportation workers.	17	–
Conveyor operators and tenders.	4	–
Crane and tower operators.	62	4.0
Dredge, excavating, and loading machine operators.	42	–
Hoist and winch operators.	5	–
Industrial truck and tractor operators.	537	7.4
Cleaners of vehicles and equipment.	315	15.2

See note at end of table.

Table 11. **Employed persons, by detailed occupation and gender, 2012 annual averages (continued)**
(Numbers in thousands)

Occupation	Total employed	Percent women
Laborers and freight, stock, and material movers, hand.	1,849	18.7
Machine feeders and offbearers.	27	–
Packers and packagers, hand.	431	53.1
Pumping station operators.	25	–
Refuse and recyclable material collectors.	106	6.6
Mine shuttle car operators.	1	–
Tank car, truck, and ship loaders.	4	–
Material moving workers, all other.	45	–

Note: Dash indicates no data or data that do not meet publication criteria (values not shown where base is less than 50,000).

Source: Current Population Survey, U.S. Bureau of Labor Statistics.

Table 12. **Employed women, by occupation, race, and Hispanic or Latino ethnicity, 2012 annual averages**

(Percent distribution)

Occupation	White	Black or African American	Asian	Hispanic or Latino ethnicity
Total, 16 years and older (thousands)	52,779	8,553	3,620	9,235
Percent	100.0	100.0	100.0	100.0
Management, professional, and related occupations.	42.6	34.3	46.8	25.9
Management, business, and financial operations occupations. .	15.2	11.9	16.2	9.5
Professional and related occupations.	27.4	22.4	30.6	16.4
Service occupations.	20.0	28.0	22.3	32.2
Sales and office occupations.	31.2	29.7	24.3	30.9
Sales and related occupations.	11.3	11.2	10.6	12.1
Office and administrative support occupations.	20.0	18.5	13.7	18.8
Natural resources, construction, and maintenance occupations. .	.9	.7	.4	1.5
Farming, fishing, and forestry occupations.	.4	.2	.2	1.1
Construction and extraction occupations.	.3	.2	.1	.3
Installation, maintenance, and repair occupations.	.2	.3	.1	.2
Production, transportation, and material moving occupations. . . .	5.2	7.2	6.2	9.5
Production occupations.	3.3	4.3	5.1	6.2
Transportation and material moving occupations.	1.9	2.9	1.1	3.3

Note: Women whose ethnicity is identified as Hispanic or Latino may be of any race.

Source: Current Population Survey, U.S. Bureau of Labor Statistics.

Table 13. **Employed persons, by industry and gender, 2011 and 2012 annual averages**

(Numbers in thousands)

Industry and gender	Year			
	2011		2012	
	Number	Percent	Number	Percent
Total				
Total, 16 years and older................................	139,869	100.0	142,469	100.0
Agriculture, forestry, fishing, and hunting	2,254	1.6	2,186	1.5
Mining, quarrying, and oil and gas extraction	817	.6	957	.7
Construction	9,039	6.5	8,964	6.3
Manufacturing	14,336	10.2	14,686	10.3
Durable goods	9,007	6.4	9,244	6.5
Nondurable goods	5,329	3.8	5,443	3.8
Wholesale and retail trade	19,726	14.1	19,876	14.0
Wholesale trade	3,798	2.7	3,694	2.6
Retail trade	15,927	11.4	16,182	11.4
Transportation and utilities	7,200	5.1	7,271	5.1
Transportation and warehousing	5,957	4.3	6,082	4.3
Utilities	1,243	.9	1,190	.8
Information	3,150	2.3	2,971	2.1
Financial activities	9,386	6.7	9,590	6.7
Finance and insurance	6,613	4.7	6,786	4.8
Real estate and rental and leasing	2,773	2.0	2,804	2.0
Professional and business services	15,819	11.3	16,539	11.6
Professional and technical services	9,461	6.8	9,913	7.0
Management, administrative, and waste services..................	6,358	4.5	6,626	4.7
Education and health services	31,867	22.8	32,350	22.7
Educational services	12,965	9.3	12,945	9.1
Health care and social assistance	18,902	13.5	19,405	13.6
Hospitals	6,315	4.5	6,113	4.3
Health services, except hospitals	9,367	6.7	10,009	7.0
Social assistance	3,221	2.3	3,283	2.3
Leisure and hospitality	12,697	9.1	13,193	9.3
Arts, entertainment, and recreation	2,922	2.1	3,022	2.1
Accommodation and food services	9,775	7.0	10,171	7.1
Other services	6,724	4.8	7,168	5.0
Other services, except private households	6,002	4.3	6,430	4.5
Private households	722	.5	738	.5
Public administration	6,853	4.9	6,717	4.7

Table 13. **Employed persons, by industry and gender, 2011 and 2012 annual averages (continued)**

(Numbers in thousands)

Industry and gender	Year			
	2011		2012	
	Number	Percent	Number	Percent
Women				
Total, 16 years and older..	65,579	100.0	66,914	100.0
Agriculture, forestry, fishing, and hunting	556	.8	560	.8
Mining, quarrying, and oil and gas extraction	99	.2	126	.2
Construction	828	1.3	802	1.2
Manufacturing	4,108	6.3	4,255	6.4
Durable goods	2,230	3.4	2,311	3.5
Nondurable goods	1,878	2.9	1,943	2.9
Wholesale and retail trade	8,826	13.5	8,871	13.3
Wholesale trade	1,083	1.7	1,056	1.6
Retail trade	7,742	11.8	7,815	11.7
Transportation and utilities	1,625	2.5	1,691	2.5
Transportation and warehousing	1,349	2.1	1,413	2.1
Utilities	276	.4	278	.4
Information	1,267	1.9	1,134	1.7
Financial activities	5,132	7.8	5,108	7.6
Finance and insurance	3,811	5.8	3,804	5.7
Real estate and rental and leasing	1,320	2.0	1,303	1.9
Professional and business services	6,480	9.9	6,798	10.2
Professional and technical services	4,023	6.1	4,281	6.4
Management, administrative, and waste services................	2,457	3.7	2,517	3.8
Education and health services	23,706	36.1	24,087	36.0
Educational services	8,870	13.5	8,877	13.3
Health care and social assistance	14,836	22.6	15,209	22.7
Hospitals	4,786	7.3	4,677	7.0
Health services, except hospitals	7,314	11.2	7,744	11.6
Social assistance	2,737	4.2	2,789	4.2
Leisure and hospitality	6,397	9.8	6,706	10.0
Arts, entertainment, and recreation	1,324	2.0	1,375	2.1
Accommodation and food services	5,073	7.7	5,331	8.0
Other services	3,494	5.3	3,728	5.6
Other services, except private households	2,850	4.3	3,072	4.6
Private households	644	1.0	656	1.0
Public administration	3,060	4.7	3,048	4.6

Table 13. **Employed persons, by industry and gender, 2011 and 2012 annual averages (continued)**

(Numbers in thousands)

Industry and gender	Year			
	2011		2012	
	Number	Percent	Number	Percent
Men				
Total, 16 years and older....................................	74,290	100.0	75,555	100.0
Agriculture, forestry, fishing, and hunting	1,698	2.3	1,626	2.2
Mining, quarrying, and oil and gas extraction	718	1.0	831	1.1
Construction	8,211	11.1	8,162	10.8
Manufacturing	10,228	13.8	10,432	13.8
Durable goods	6,777	9.1	6,932	9.2
Nondurable goods	3,451	4.6	3,499	4.6
Wholesale and retail trade	10,900	14.7	11,004	14.6
Wholesale trade	2,715	3.7	2,638	3.5
Retail trade	8,185	11.0	8,367	11.1
Transportation and utilities	5,575	7.5	5,581	7.4
Transportation and warehousing	4,608	6.2	4,669	6.2
Utilities	967	1.3	912	1.2
Information	1,883	2.5	1,838	2.4
Financial activities	4,255	5.7	4,482	5.9
Finance and insurance	2,802	3.8	2,981	3.9
Real estate and rental and leasing	1,453	2.0	1,501	2.0
Professional and business services	9,338	12.6	9,741	12.9
Professional and technical services	5,438	7.3	5,632	7.5
Management, administrative, and waste services.................	3,901	5.3	4,109	5.4
Education and health services	8,160	11.0	8,263	10.9
Educational services	4,095	5.5	4,068	5.4
Health care and social assistance	4,066	5.5	4,196	5.6
Hospitals	1,529	2.1	1,436	1.9
Health services, except hospitals	2,053	2.8	2,265	3.0
Social assistance	484	0.7	494	0.7
Leisure and hospitality	6,300	8.5	6,487	8.6
Arts, entertainment, and recreation	1,599	2.2	1,647	2.2
Accommodation and food services	4,702	6.3	4,840	6.4
Other services	3,230	4.3	3,439	4.6
Other services, except private households	3,152	4.2	3,357	4.4
Private households	78	.1	82	.1
Public administration	3,793	5.1	3,669	4.9

Source: Current Population Survey, U.S. Bureau of Labor Statistics.

Table 14. **Employed persons, by detailed industry and gender, 2012 annual averages**

(Numbers in thousands)

Industry	Total employed	Percent women
Total, 16 years and older...	142,469	47.0
Agriculture, forestry, fishing, and hunting..	2,186	25.6
Crop production...	955	25.2
Animal production..	899	26.2
Forestry, except logging...	49	–
Logging..	82	8.8
Fishing, hunting, and trapping..	42	–
Support activities for agriculture and forestry.................	160	35.5
Mining, quarrying, and oil and gas extraction..............................	957	13.2
Oil and gas extraction..	92	23.3
Coal mining...	97	5.9
Metal ore mining..	45	–
Nonmetallic mineral mining and quarrying.......................	88	13.5
Not specified type of mining...	15	–
Support activities for mining...	620	12.8
Construction..	8,964	9.0
Manufacturing...	14,686	29.0
Durable goods...	9,244	25.0
Nonmetallic mineral products..	403	21.0
Pottery, ceramics, and related product manufacturing....	32	–
Structural clay product manufacturing.......................	28	–
Glass and glass product manufacturing....................	150	29.2
Cement, concrete, lime, and gypsum product manufacturing....	136	7.1
Miscellaneous nonmetallic mineral product manufacturing....	57	16.7
Primary metals and fabricated metal product manufacturing....	1,657	17.7
Iron and steel mills and steel product manufacturing....	288	12.8
Aluminum production and processing.........................	67	16.7
Nonferrous metal, except aluminum, production and processing....	68	11.8
Foundries..	87	13.5
Metal forgings and stampings..................................	49	–
Cutlery and hand tool manufacturing.........................	44	–
Structural metals and tanks and shipping container manufacturing....	362	18.6
Machine shops; turned products; screw, nut, and bolt manufacturing....	294	10.4
Coating, engraving, heat treating and allied activities....	68	22.9
Ordnance...	44	–
Miscellaneous fabricated metal product manufacturing....	269	25.0
Not specified metal industries...................................	17	–
Machinery manufacturing...	1,295	21.4
Agricultural implement manufacturing........................	125	20.0
Construction, and mining and oil and gas field machinery manufacturing....	161	15.6
Commercial and service industry machinery manufacturing....	86	34.1
Metalworking machinery manufacturing.....................	155	14.7
Engines, turbines, and power transmission equipment manufacturing....	73	21.3
Machinery manufacturing, n.e.c................................	690	23.1
Not specified machinery manufacturing.....................	6	–
Computers and electronic product manufacturing.............	1,272	30.9
Computer and peripheral equipment manufacturing.....	251	34.1
Communications, and audio and video equipment manufacturing....	129	23.8
Navigational, measuring, electromedical, and control instruments manufacturing....	224	30.3
Electronic component and product manufacturing, n.e.c....	668	31.3

See note at end of table.

Table 14. **Employed persons, by detailed industry and gender, 2012 annual averages (continued)**

(Numbers in thousands)

Industry	Total employed	Percent women
Electrical equipment and appliances manufacturing..	390	31.7
Household appliance manufacturing...	70	42.3
Electrical lighting and electrical equipment manufacturing, and other electrical component manufacturing, n.e.c....................................	321	29.4
Transportation equipment manufacturing...	2,061	22.3
Motor vehicles and motor vehicle equipment manufacturing.........................	1,034	24.2
Aircraft and parts manufacturing...	385	21.3
Aerospace product and parts manufacturing...	427	22.9
Railroad rolling stock manufacturing..	29	–
Ship and boat building..	150	10.2
Other transportation equipment manufacturing.....................................	36	–
Wood products manufacturing..	388	14.9
Sawmills and wood preservation..	126	10.3
Veneer, plywood, and engineered wood products..................................	32	–
Prefabricated wood buildings and mobile homes..................................	32	–
Miscellaneous wood products..	199	16.7
Furniture and fixtures manufacturing...	410	24.9
Miscellaneous manufacturing..	1,366	38.1
Medical equipment and supplies manufacturing....................................	583	42.4
Sporting and athletic goods, and doll, toy and game manufacturing............	108	35.5
Miscellaneous manufacturing, n.e.c...	490	35.6
Not specified manufacturing industries..	186	33.1
Nondurable goods manufacturing..	5,443	35.7
Food manufacturing...	1,706	40.6
Animal food, grain, and oilseed milling..	151	26.9
Sugar and confectionery products..	72	42.1
Fruit and vegetable preserving and specialty foods manufacturing.............	132	37.0
Dairy product manufacturing...	150	28.1
Animal slaughtering and processing..	480	37.1
Retail bakeries..	279	61.9
Bakeries, except retail..	183	37.5
Seafood and other miscellaneous foods, n.e.c.....................................	190	43.3
Not specified food industries..	70	41.1
Beverages and tobacco products manufacturing.....................................	272	26.4
Beverage manufacturing...	257	26.2
Tobacco manufacturing...	15	–
Textiles, apparel, and leather manufacturing...	597	52.9
Fiber, yarn, and thread mills..	9	–
Fabric mills, except knitting mills..	103	44.0
Textile and fabric finishing and coating mills......................................	23	–
Carpet and rug mills..	50	43.5
Textile product mills, except carpet and rug.......................................	93	52.5
Knitting fabric mills and apparel knitting mills.....................................	24	–
Cut and sew apparel manufacturing..	223	62.0
Apparel accessories and other apparel manufacturing...........................	8	–
Footwear manufacturing..	35	–
Leather tanning and finishing and other allied products manufacturing.......	30	–
Paper manufacturing and printing...	883	28.2
Pulp, paper, and paperboard mills..	189	16.7
Paperboard containers and boxes..	94	17.8
Miscellaneous paper and pulp products...	85	34.8
Printing and related support activities...	515	33.2
Petroleum and coal products manufacturing..	207	17.7
Petroleum refining..	191	17.6

See note at end of table.

Table 14. **Employed persons, by detailed industry and gender, 2012 annual averages (continued)**

(Numbers in thousands)

Industry	Total employed	Percent women
Miscellaneous petroleum and coal products...	16	–
Chemicals manufacturing...	1,286	33.4
Resin, synthetic rubber and fbers, and filaments manufacturing..............................	206	30.0
Agricultural chemical manufacturing...	31	–
Pharmaceutical and medicine manufacturing...	451	46.6
Paint, coating, and adhesive manufacturing...	56	18.5
Soap, cleaning compound, and cosmetics manufacturing..	140	53.0
Industrial and miscellaneous chemicals..	401	16.6
Plastics and rubber products manufacturing..	491	30.2
Plastics product manufacturing..	331	32.0
Tire manufacturing...	79	25.1
Rubber product, except tire, manufacturing...	80	28.0
Wholesale and retail trade..	19,876	44.6
Wholesale trade..	3,694	28.6
Motor vehicles, parts and supplies, merchant wholesalers..............................	185	23.7
Furniture and home furnishings, merchant wholesalers...	65	37.1
Lumber and other construction materials, merchant wholesalers...........................	157	21.4
Professional and commercial equipment and supplies, merchant wholesalers...........	364	38.0
Metals and minerals, except petroleum, merchant wholesalers..........................	47	–
Electrical and electronic goods, merchant wholesalers.......................................	207	26.2
Hardware, plumbing and heating equipment, and supplies, merchant wholesalers..........	135	20.1
Machinery, equipment, and supplies, merchant wholesalers................................	379	25.2
Recyclable material, merchant wholesalers..	124	15.8
Miscellaneous durable goods, merchant wholesalers..	114	28.7
Paper and paper products, merchant wholesalers..	52	29.6
Drugs, sundries, and chemical and allied products, merchant wholesalers...........	226	45.1
Apparel, fabrics, and notions, merchant wholesalers...	104	49.5
Groceries and related products, merchant wholesalers.......................................	839	23.4
Farm product raw materials, merchant wholesalers..	64	36.7
Petroleum and petroleum products, merchant wholesalers..................................	149	23.5
Alcoholic beverages, merchant wholesalers...	121	19.0
Farm supplies, merchant wholesalers..	50	25.0
Miscellaneous nondurable goods, merchant wholesalers....................................	188	40.4
Wholesale electronic markets, agents and brokers...	85	39.4
Not specified wholesale trade..	38	–
Retail trade...	16,182	48.3
Automobile dealers..	1,237	19.7
Other motor vehicle dealers..	126	17.3
Auto parts, accessories, and tire stores..	496	15.9
Furniture and home furnishings stores...	501	40.2
Household appliance stores...	66	29.8
Radio, TV, and computer stores...	578	28.8
Building material and supplies dealers...	895	30.1
Hardware stores...	245	26.5
Lawn and garden equipment and supplies stores...	280	29.8
Grocery stores..	2,792	49.3
Specialty food stores...	293	48.2
Beer, wine, and liquor stores..	156	36.9
Pharmacies and drug stores..	871	63.6
Health and personal care, except drug, stores...	327	67.5
Gasoline stations..	484	50.6
Clothing stores...	1,008	76.8

See note at end of table.

Table 14. **Employed persons, by detailed industry and gender, 2012 annual averages (continued)**

(Numbers in thousands)

Industry	Total employed	Percent women
Shoe stores	183	50.3
Jewelry, luggage, and leather goods stores	199	66.3
Sporting goods, camera, and hobby and toy stores	461	43.6
Sewing, needlework, and piece goods stores	68	78.9
Music stores	59	28.7
Book stores and news dealers	150	52.9
Department stores and discount stores	2,205	60.2
Miscellaneous general merchandise stores	506	58.5
Retail florists	97	76.5
Office supplies and stationery stores	142	38.6
Used merchandise stores	255	62.3
Gift, novelty, and souvenir shops	143	73.7
Miscellaneous retail stores	459	53.7
Electronic shopping	168	41.7
Electronic auctions	23	–
Mail order houses	78	65.3
Vending machine operators	42	–
Fuel dealers	81	22.1
Other direct selling establishments	192	73.7
Not specified retail trade	316	51.7
Transportation and utilities	7,271	23.2
Transportation and warehousing	6,082	23.2
Air transportation	559	36.0
Rail transportation	254	9.6
Water transportation	56	16.8
Truck transportation	1,784	11.7
Bus service and urban transit	472	38.1
Taxi and limousine service	225	11.5
Pipeline transportation	59	26.0
Scenic and sightseeing transportation	37	–
Services incidental to transportation	843	24.3
Postal Service	704	40.2
Couriers and messengers	671	19.6
Warehousing and storage	417	28.2
Utilities	1,190	23.3
Electric power generation, transmission, and distribution	620	23.4
Natural gas distribution	111	29.4
Electric and gas, and other combinations	83	34.8
Water, steam, air-conditioning, and irrigation systems	237	20.9
Sewage treatment facilities	121	13.8
Not specified utilities	17	–
Information	2,971	38.2
Newspaper publishers	283	44.7
Periodical, book, and directory publishers	252	52.3
Software publishers	67	35.0
Motion pictures and video industries	370	30.9
Sound recording industries	33	–
Radio and television broadcasting and cable subscription programming	547	32.4
Internet publishing and broadcasting and web search portals	60	36.6
Wired telecommunications carriers	523	27.7
Other telecommunications services	487	33.9

See note at end of table.

Table 14. Employed persons, by detailed industry and gender, 2012 annual averages (continued)

(Numbers in thousands)

Industry	Total employed	Percent women
Data processing, hosting, and related services...	104	43.0
Libraries and archives..	210	76.1
Other information services...	35	–
Financial activities...	9,590	53.3
Finance and insurance..	6,786	56.1
Banking and related activities..	2,112	60.6
Savings institutions, including credit unions...	239	74.7
Nondepository credit and related activities...	875	53.3
Securities, commodities, funds, trusts, and other financial investments........	1,122	38.6
Insurance carriers and related activities...	2,437	59.4
Real estate and rental and leasing..	2,804	46.5
Real estate...	2,409	49.6
Rental and leasing services...	395	27.4
Automotive equipment rental and leasing..	172	27.5
Video tape and disk rental..	18	–
Other consumer goods rental...	103	29.1
Commercial, industrial, and other intangible assets rental and leasing......	101	21.2
Professional and business services...	16,539	41.1
Professional and technical services..	9,913	43.2
Legal services..	1,714	56.5
Accounting, tax preparation, bookkeeping, and payroll services....................	1,044	60.4
Architectural, engineering, and related services...	1,525	25.7
Specialized design services..	371	57.9
Computer systems design and related services..	2,092	24.5
Management, scientific, and technical consulting services.............................	1,415	41.7
Scientific research and development services...	510	48.1
Advertising and related services...	559	50.2
Veterinary services..	311	77.1
Other professional, scientific, and technical services.....................................	373	56.1
Management, administrative, and waste services...	6,626	38.0
Management of companies and enterprises...	187	49.7
Employment services...	1,037	52.1
Business support services...	793	62.9
Travel arrangement and reservation services...	268	61.7
Investigation and security services...	782	24.2
Services to buildings and dwellings..	1,422	52.4
Landscaping services..	1,327	7.4
Other administrative and other support services..	293	38.7
Waste management and remediation services..	518	14.4
Education and health services...	32,350	74.5
Educational services...	12,945	68.6
Elementary and secondary schools...	8,491	75.8
Colleges and universities, including junior colleges..	3,609	53.1
Business, technical, and trade schools and training..	121	48.2
Other schools, instruction, and educational services......................................	723	64.2
Health care and social assistance...	19,405	78.4
Hospitals...	6,113	76.5

See note at end of table.

Table 14. Employed persons, by detailed industry and gender, 2012 annual averages (continued)

(Numbers in thousands)

Industry	Total employed	Percent women
Health services, except hospitals..	10,009	77.4
Offices of physicians..	1,502	76.1
Offices of dentists..	835	81.6
Offices of chiropractors..	134	61.8
Offices of optometrists..	122	72.6
Offices of other health practitioners..	257	73.2
Outpatient care centers..	1,285	74.6
Home health care services..	1,040	87.6
Other health care services..	2,392	71.9
Nursing care facilities..	1,726	84.7
Residential care facilities, without nursing..	717	71.2
Social assistance..	3,283	84.9
Individual and family services..	1,459	78.9
Community food and housing, and emergency services..	118	74.3
Vocational rehabilitation services..	158	52.7
Child day care services..	1,549	94.8
Leisure and hospitality..	13,193	50.8
Arts, entertainment, and recreation..	3,022	45.5
Independent artists, performing arts, spectator sports, and related industries.................	824	42.6
Museums, art galleries, historical sites, and similar institutions................................	340	43.7
Bowling centers..	44	–
Other amusement, gambling, and recreation industries................................	1,813	47.1
Accommodation and food services..	10,171	52.4
Accommodation..	1,426	57.4
Traveler accommodation..	1,332	57.6
Recreational vehicle parks and camps, and rooming and boarding houses................	94	55.5
Food services and drinking places..	8,745	51.6
Restaurants and other food services..	8,484	51.5
Drinking places, alcoholic beverages..	261	54.1
Other services..	7,168	52.0
Other services, except private households..	6,430	47.8
Repair and maintenance..	2,146	12.1
Automotive repair and maintenance..	1,237	10.0
Car washes..	171	13.5
Electronic and precision equipment repair and maintenance................................	179	12.2
Commercial and industrial machinery and equipment repair and maintenance............	360	8.6
Personal and household goods repair and maintenance................................	191	30.6
Footwear and leather goods repair..	8	–
Personal and laundry services..	2,379	71.8
Barber shops..	121	28.7
Beauty salons..	987	90.0
Nail salons and other personal care services..	466	74.0
Drycleaning and laundry services..	337	57.7
Funeral homes, cemeteries, and crematories..	124	34.0
Other personal services..	344	59.3
Membership associations and organizations..	1,904	58.0
Religious organizations..	1,059	51.7
Civic, social, advocacy organizations, and grantmaking and giving services..........	638	69.7
Labor unions..	50	32.1
Business, professional, political, and similar organizations................................	157	61.7
Private households..	738	88.9

See note at end of table.

Table 14. **Employed persons, by detailed industry and gender, 2012 annual averages (continued)**

(Numbers in thousands)

Industry	Total employed	Percent women
Public administration..	6,717	45.4
Executive offices and legislative bodies..	1,031	53.3
Public finance activities..	373	65.4
Other general government and support..	133	37.7
Justice, public order, and safety activities..	2,690	33.3
Administration of human resource programs...	940	70.5
Administration of environmental quality and housing programs....................	298	41.9
Administration of economic programs and space research..........................	561	46.7
National security and international affairs..	690	37.3

n.e.c. = not elsewhere classified.

Note: Dash indicates no data or data that do not meet publication criteria (values not shown where base is less than 50,000)

Source: Current Population Survey, U.S. Bureau of Labor Statistics.

Table 15. **Employed women, by industry, race, and Hispanic or Latino ethnicity, 2012 annual averages**
(Percent distribution)

Industry	White	Black or African American	Asian	Hispanic or Latino ethnicity
Total, 16 years and older (thousands).............	52,779	8,553	3,620	9,235
Percent...	100.0	100.0	100.0	100.0
Agriculture and related industries	1.0	0.1	0.4	1.1
Mining, quarrying, and oil and gas extraction	.2	.1	.1	.2
Construction	1.4	.5	.7	.9
Manufacturing	6.3	5.4	9.0	7.8
Durable goods manufacturing	3.4	2.8	5.4	3.2
Nondurable goods manufacturing	2.9	2.6	3.6	4.5
Wholesale and retail trade	13.5	11.8	12.3	14.1
Wholesale trade	1.7	.9	1.7	1.7
Retail trade	11.8	11.0	10.5	12.4
Transportation and utilities	2.4	3.7	2.0	2.7
Transportation and warehousing	1.9	3.2	1.9	2.4
Utilities	.4	.5	.2	.3
Information	1.7	1.7	1.9	1.2
Financial activities	7.9	6.6	7.0	6.7
Finance and insurance	5.8	5.3	5.6	5.0
Real estate and rental and leasing	2.1	1.3	1.4	1.7
Professional and business services	10.4	8.4	11.4	10.5
Professional and technical services	6.7	3.8	9.2	4.0
Management, administrative, and waste services...	3.7	4.6	2.1	6.6
Education and health services	35.6	41.4	31.0	30.1
Educational services	14.0	11.5	8.5	10.0
Health care and social assistance	21.6	29.9	22.5	20.1
Hospitals	6.7	8.7	8.1	4.6
Health services, except hospitals	11.0	15.2	11.0	10.2
Social assistance	3.9	6.0	3.4	5.3
Leisure and hospitality	9.9	8.9	11.7	14.5
Arts, entertainment, and recreation	2.1	1.4	2.2	1.7
Accommodation and food services	7.8	7.6	9.4	12.8
Other services	5.5	4.3	9.1	6.8
Other services, except private households	4.5	3.7	8.3	4.1
Private households	1.0	.6	.7	2.7
Public administration	4.1	7.0	3.6	3.6

Note: Women whose ethnicity is identified as Hispanic or Latino may be of any race.

Source: Current Population Survey, U.S. Bureau of Labor Statistics.

Table 16. **Median usual weekly earnings of full-time wage and salary workers, in current dollars, by race, Hispanic or Latino ethnicity, and gender, 1979–2012 annual averages**

Year	Total					Women				
	Total	White	Black or African American	Asian	Hispanic or Latino ethnicity	Total	White	Black or African American	Asian	Hispanic or Latino ethnicity
1979.......	$241	$248	$199	–	$194	$182	$184	$169	–	$157
1980.......	262	269	212	–	209	201	203	185	–	172
1981.......	284	291	235	–	223	219	221	206	–	190
1982.......	302	310	245	–	240	239	242	217	–	203
1983.......	313	320	261	–	250	252	254	232	–	215
1984.......	326	336	269	–	259	265	268	241	–	223
1985.......	344	356	277	–	270	277	281	252	–	230
1986.......	359	371	291	–	277	291	294	264	–	241
1987.......	374	384	301	–	285	303	307	276	–	251
1988.......	385	395	314	–	290	315	318	288	–	260
1989.......	399	409	319	–	298	328	334	301	–	269
1990.......	412	424	329	–	304	346	353	308	–	278
1991.......	426	442	348	–	312	366	373	323	–	292
1992.......	440	458	357	–	321	380	387	335	–	302
1993.......	459	475	369	–	331	393	401	348	–	313
1994.......	467	484	371	–	324	399	408	346	–	305
1995.......	479	494	383	–	329	406	415	355	–	305
1996.......	490	506	387	–	339	418	428	362	–	316
1997.......	503	519	400	–	351	431	444	375	–	318
1998.......	523	545	426	–	370	456	468	400	–	337
1999.......	549	573	445	–	385	473	483	409	–	348
2000.......	576	590	474	$615	399	493	502	429	$547	366
2001.......	596	610	491	639	417	512	522	454	563	388
2002.......	608	623	498	658	424	529	547	473	566	397
2003.......	620	636	514	693	440	552	567	491	598	410
2004.......	638	657	525	708	456	573	584	505	613	419
2005.......	651	672	520	753	471	585	596	499	665	429
2006.......	671	690	554	784	486	600	609	519	699	440
2007.......	695	716	569	830	503	614	626	533	731	473
2008.......	722	742	589	861	529	638	654	554	753	501
2009.......	739	757	601	880	541	657	669	582	779	509
2010.......	747	765	611	855	535	669	684	592	773	508
2011.......	756	775	615	866	549	684	703	595	751	518
2012.......	768	792	621	920	568	691	710	599	770	521

See note at end of table.

Table 16. Median usual weekly earnings of full-time wage and salary workers in current dollars by race, Hispanic or Latino ethnicity, and gender, 1979–2012 annual averages (continued)

Year	Men					Women's earnings as a percentage of men's				
	Total	White	Black or African American	Asian	Hispanic or Latino ethnicity	Total	White	Black or African American	Asian	Hispanic or Latino ethnicity
1979......	$292	$298	$227	–	$219	62.3	61.7	74.4	–	71.7
1980......	313	320	244	–	234	64.2	63.4	75.8	–	73.5
1981......	340	350	268	–	251	64.4	63.1	76.9	–	75.7
1982......	364	375	278	–	269	65.7	64.5	78.1	–	75.5
1983......	379	387	294	–	274	66.5	65.6	78.9	–	78.5
1984......	392	401	303	–	287	67.6	66.8	79.5	–	77.7
1985......	407	418	305	–	296	68.1	67.2	82.6	–	77.7
1986......	419	433	319	–	299	69.5	67.9	82.8	–	80.6
1987......	434	450	327	–	306	69.8	68.2	84.4	–	82.0
1988......	449	465	348	–	308	70.2	68.4	82.8	–	84.4
1989......	468	482	348	–	315	70.1	69.3	86.5	–	85.4
1990......	481	494	361	–	318	71.9	71.5	85.3	–	87.4
1991......	493	506	375	–	323	74.2	73.7	86.1	–	90.4
1992......	501	514	380	–	339	75.8	75.3	88.2	–	89.1
1993......	510	524	392	–	346	77.1	76.5	88.8	–	90.5
1994......	522	547	400	–	343	76.4	74.6	86.5	–	88.9
1995......	538	566	411	–	350	75.5	73.3	86.4	–	87.1
1996......	557	580	412	–	356	75.0	73.8	87.9	–	88.8
1997......	579	595	432	–	371	74.4	74.6	86.8	–	85.7
1998......	598	615	468	–	390	76.3	76.1	85.5	–	86.4
1999......	618	638	488	–	406	76.5	75.7	83.8	–	85.7
2000......	641	662	510	$685	417	76.9	75.8	84.1	79.9	87.8
2001......	670	689	529	732	440	76.4	75.8	85.8	76.9	88.2
2002......	679	702	524	756	451	77.9	77.9	90.3	74.9	88.0
2003......	695	715	555	772	464	79.4	79.3	88.5	77.5	88.4
2004......	713	732	569	802	480	80.4	79.8	88.8	76.4	87.3
2005......	722	743	559	825	489	81.0	80.2	89.3	80.6	87.7
2006......	743	761	591	882	505	80.8	80.0	87.8	79.3	87.1
2007......	766	788	600	936	520	80.2	79.4	88.8	78.1	91.0
2008......	798	825	620	966	559	79.9	79.3	89.4	78.0	89.6
2009......	819	845	621	952	569	80.2	79.2	93.7	81.8	89.5
2010......	824	850	633	936	560	81.2	80.5	93.5	82.6	90.7
2011......	832	856	653	970	571	82.2	82.1	91.1	77.4	90.7
2012......	854	879	665	1,055	592	80.9	80.8	90.1	73.0	88.0

Note: The comparability of historical labor force data has been affected at various times by methodological and conceptual changes in the Current Population Survey (CPS). For an explanation, see the historical comparability section of the household data technical documentation provided at www.bls.gov/cps/documentation.htm#comp. Beginning in 2003, estimates for the race groups shown (White, Black or African American, and Asian) include people who selected that race group only; people who selected more than one race group are not included. Prior to 2003, people who reported more than one race were included in the group they identified as the main race. Data for 2000 to 2002 are for the category Asians and Pacific Islanders. Starting in 2003, Asians constituted a separate category. For more information, see the historical comparability documentation. Persons whose ethnicity is identified as Hispanic or Latino may be of any race. Dashes indicate that data for Asians were not tabulated prior to 2000.

Source: Current Population Survey, U.S. Bureau of Labor Statistics.

Table 17. **Median usual weekly earnings of full-time wage and salary workers 25 years and older, by educational attainment and gender, 2012 annual averages**

Educational attainment and gender	Total employed (in thousands)	Median weekly earnings
Total		
Total..	93,719	$815
Less than a high school diploma	7,010	471
High school graduate or more..............	86,709	857
High school graduates, no college......	25,239	652
Some college or associate's degree.....	25,826	749
Some college, no degree................	15,470	727
Associate's degree.........................	10,357	785
Occupational program....................	4,554	775
Academic program.......................	5,803	795
College graduates, total....................	35,644	1,165
Bachelor's degree.........................	22,715	1,066
Master's degree............................	9,519	1,300
Professional degree.......................	1,612	1,735
Doctoral degree...........................	1,799	1,624
Women		
Total..	41,597	727
Less than a high school diploma...........	2,236	386
High school graduate or more..............	39,361	749
High school graduates, no college......	10,152	561
Some college or associate's degree.....	12,310	659
Some college, no degree................	7,025	634
Associate's degree.........................	5,285	697
Occupational program....................	2,158	670
Academic program.......................	3,128	714
College graduates, total....................	16,899	1,001
Bachelor's degree.........................	10,697	931
Master's degree............................	4,934	1,122
Professional degree.......................	599	1,411
Doctoral degree...........................	669	1,413

Table 17. **Median usual weekly earnings of full-time wage and salary workers 25 years and older, by educational attainment and gender, 2012 annual averages (continued)**

Educational attainment and gender	Total employed (in thousands)	Median weekly earnings
Men		
Total...	52,122	$910
Less than a high school diploma...........	4,773	508
High school graduate or more..............	47,349	961
High school graduates, no college......	15,087	735
Some college or associate's degree.....	13,517	857
Some college, no degree................	8,445	826
Associate's degree........................	5,072	905
Occupational program....................	2,396	892
Academic program.......................	2,675	918
College graduates, total....................	18,745	1,371
Bachelor's degree..........................	12,018	1,246
Master's degree...........................	4,585	1,545
Professional degree.......................	1,012	1,896
Doctoral degree...........................	1,130	1,778

Source: Current Population Survey, U.S. Bureau of Labor Statistics.

Table 18. **Median usual weekly earnings of full-time wage and salary workers by detailed occupation and gender,**
2012 annual averages

Occupation	Total		Women		Men		Women's earnings as a percentage of men's
	Number of workers (thousands)	Median weekly earnings	Total employed	Median weekly earnings	Total employed	Median weekly earnings	
Total, 16 years and older...	102,749	$768	45,462	$691	57,286	$854	80.9
Management, professional, and related occupations...............	40,984	1,108	21,059	951	19,926	1,328	71.6
Management, business, and financial operations occupations.................................	16,991	1,171	7,869	993	9,121	1,387	71.6
Management occupations.............................	11,547	1,248	4,765	1,036	6,783	1,428	72.5
Chief executives.............................	1,004	2,060	265	1,730	739	2,275	76.0
General and operations managers................	983	1,264	278	971	705	1,436	67.6
Legislators...	7	(^{1})	3	(^{1})	4	(^{1})	(^{2})
Advertising and promotions managers........................	65	1,334	29	(^{1})	36	(^{1})	(^{2})
Marketing and sales managers........................	916	1,396	402	1,110	514	1,640	67.7
Public relations and fundraising managers..................	56	1,237	39	(^{1})	17	(^{1})	(^{2})
Administrative services managers..................	133	1,103	57	1,038	76	1,212	85.6
Computer and information systems managers..............	568	1,672	145	1,527	423	1,740	87.8
Financial managers........................	1,125	1,169	616	988	509	1,405	70.3
Compensation and benefits managers........................	16	(^{1})	9	(^{1})	7	(^{1})	(^{2})
Human resources managers........................	216	1,271	160	1,208	56	1,447	83.5
Training and development managers........................	33	(^{1})	17	(^{1})	16	(^{1})	(^{2})
Industrial production managers........................	219	1,183	34	(^{1})	185	1,181	(^{2})
Purchasing managers........................	204	1,319	99	1,072	104	1,467	73.1
Transportation, storage, and distribution managers........	276	953	36	(^{1})	240	938	(^{2})
Farmers, ranchers, and other agricultural managers........	104	708	14	(^{1})	89	699	(^{2})
Construction managers........................	460	1,208	35	(^{1})	425	1,233	(^{2})
Education administrators........................	704	1,255	454	1,052	250	1,566	67.2
Architectural and engineering managers....................	111	2,122	9	(^{1})	101	2,116	(^{2})
Food service managers........................	678	689	327	601	351	744	80.8
Funeral service managers........................	8	(^{1})	4	(^{1})	5	(^{1})	(^{2})
Gaming managers........................	21	(^{1})	6	(^{1})	15	(^{1})	(^{2})
Lodging managers........................	100	774	47	(^{1})	53	1,131	(^{2})
Medical and health services managers..................	502	1,280	358	1,190	144	1,544	77.1
Natural sciences managers........................	18	(^{1})	11	(^{1})	7	(^{1})	(^{2})
Postmasters and mail superintendents..................	35	(^{1})	21	(^{1})	14	(^{1})	(^{2})
Property, real estate, and community association managers............	353	907	200	817	153	1,045	78.2
Social and community service managers..................	260	947	184	883	76	1,151	76.7
Emergency management directors..................	5	(^{1})	2	(^{1})	3	(^{1})	(^{2})
Managers, all other........................	2,367	1,258	902	1,078	1,465	1,409	76.5
Business and financial operations occupations................	5,443	1,058	3,105	952	2,339	1,274	74.7
Agents and business managers of artists, performers, and athletes........................	31	(^{1})	16	(^{1})	15	(^{1})	(^{2})
Buyers and purchasing agents, farm products..............	8	(^{1})	2	(^{1})	6	(^{1})	(^{2})
Wholesale and retail buyers, except farm products..........	141	850	75	847	66	853	99.3
Purchasing agents, except wholesale, retail, and farm products........................	239	987	130	942	109	1,057	89.1
Claims adjusters, appraisers, examiners, and investigators........................	307	909	203	803	104	1,158	69.3
Compliance officers........................	192	1,183	91	999	101	1,304	76.6
Cost estimators........................	91	1,154	10	(^{1})	81	1,164	(^{2})
Human resource workers........................	559	994	401	944	158	1,249	75.6
Compensation, benefits, and job analysis specialits........	72	961	59	866	13	(^{1})	(^{2})
Training and development specialists........................	120	983	69	866	51	1,144	75.7
Logisticians........................	88	1,009	30	(^{1})	57	1,225	(^{2})
Management analysts........................	479	1,452	202	1,325	277	1,535	86.3
Meeting, convention, and event planners..................	86	819	72	824	15	(^{1})	(^{2})

See footnotes at end of table.

Table 18. **Median usual weekly earnings of full-time wage and salary workers by detailed occupation and gender,** 2012 annual averages (continued)

Occupation	Both sexes		Women		Men		Women's earnings as a percentage of men's
	Number of workers (thousands)	Median weekly earnings	Total employed	Median weekly earnings	Total employed	Median weekly earnings	
Fundraisers..	61	$1,058	45	(^{1})	16	(^{1})	(^{2})
Market research analysts and marketing specialists.........	175	1,148	90	$1,073	85	$1,197	89.6
Business operations specialists, all other......................	220	970	147	904	73	1,271	71.1
Accountants and auditors.................................	1,471	1,110	886	996	585	1,350	73.8
Appraisers and assessors of real estate.....................	48	(^{1})	25	(^{1})	23	(^{1})	(^{2})
Budget analysts..	52	1,207	28	(^{1})	24	(^{1})	(^{2})
Credit analysts...	33	(^{1})	18	(^{1})	15	(^{1})	(^{2})
Financial analysts..	77	1,487	30	(^{1})	48	(^{1})	(^{2})
Personal financial advisors................................	278	1,327	96	1,016	182	1,532	66.3
Insurance underwriters..	91	954	66	933	24	(^{1})	(^{2})
Financial examiners..	11	(^{1})	6	(^{1})	5	(^{1})	(^{2})
Credit counselors and loan officers..........................	310	934	181	850	130	1,074	79.1
Tax examiners, collectors, and revenue agents..............	87	937	54	849	33	(^{1})	(^{2})
Tax preparers..	48	(^{1})	25	(^{1})	24	(^{1})	(^{2})
Financial specialists, all other..............................	68	1,025	48	(^{1})	20	(^{1})	(^{2})
Professional and related occupations........................	23,993	1,053	13,189	928	10,804	1,267	73.2
Computer and mathematical occupations.....................	3,416	1,349	872	1,146	2,544	1,414	81.0
Computer and information research scientists...............	27	(^{1})	6	(^{1})	21	(^{1})	(^{2})
Computer systems analysts.................................	440	1,406	145	1,254	295	1,477	84.9
Information security analysts..............................	51	1,592	8	(^{1})	43	(^{1})	(^{2})
Computer programmers.......................................	439	1,324	100	1,148	340	1,363	84.2
Software developers, applications and systems software...	1,005	1,591	197	1,362	808	1,674	81.4
Web developers..	123	1,082	36	(^{1})	86	1,204	(^{2})
Computer support specialists................................	429	960	116	881	313	985	89.4
Database administrators......................................	97	1,376	40	(^{1})	57	1,657	(^{2})
Network and computer systems administrators..............	204	1,191	51	1,056	153	1,253	84.3
Computer network architects................................	115	1,548	11	(^{1})	104	1,569	(^{2})
Computer occupations, all other............................	288	1,110	65	887	223	1,155	76.8
Actuaries..	19	(^{1})	6	(^{1})	14	(^{1})	(^{2})
Mathematicians..	4	(^{1})	1	(^{1})	3	(^{1})	(^{2})
Operations research analysts................................	127	1,334	70	1,169	57	1,551	75.4
Statisticians...	44	(^{1})	18	(^{1})	26	(^{1})	(^{2})
Miscellaneous mathematical science occupations...........	4	(^{1})	3	(^{1})	1	(^{1})	(^{2})
Architecture and engineering occupations.....................	2,588	1,337	319	1,136	2,269	1,358	83.7
Architects, except naval.....................................	130	1,325	29	(^{1})	102	1,415	(^{2})
Surveyors, cartographers, and photogrammetrists..........	45	(^{1})	12	(^{1})	32	(^{1})	(^{2})
Aerospace engineers...	120	1,645	10	(^{1})	111	1,665	(^{2})
Agricultural engineers..	4	(^{1})	1	(^{1})	3	(^{1})	(^{2})
Biomedical engineers...	11	(^{1})	1	(^{1})	10	(^{1})	(^{2})
Chemical engineers...	71	1,509	10	(^{1})	61	1,582	(^{2})
Civil engineers..	334	1,367	47	(^{1})	287	1,428	(^{2})
Computer hardware engineers...............................	73	1,548	7	(^{1})	66	1,571	(^{2})
Electrical and electronics engineers........................	311	1,550	27	(^{1})	284	1,614	(^{2})
Environmental engineers.....................................	39	(^{1})	6	(^{1})	33	(^{1})	(^{2})
Industrial engineers, including health and safety............	202	1,393	34	(^{1})	167	1,408	(^{2})
Marine engineers and naval architects......................	10	(^{1})	2	(^{1})	7	(^{1})	(^{2})
Materials engineers...	36	(^{1})	6	(^{1})	30	(^{1})	(^{2})
Mechanical engineers...	280	1,434	10	(^{1})	270	1,442	(^{2})
Mining and geological engineers, including mining safety engineers..........................	9	(^{1})	0	(^{1})	8	(^{1})	(^{2})
Nuclear engineers...	10	(^{1})	0	(^{1})	10	(^{1})	(^{2})
Petroleum engineers..	33	(^{1})	3	(^{1})	30	(^{1})	(^{2})

See footnotes at end of table.

Table 18. **Median usual weekly earnings of full-time wage and salary workers by detailed occupation and gender,**
2012 annual averages (continued)

Occupation	Both sexes		Women		Men		Women's earnings as a percentage of men's
	Number of workers (thousands)	Median weekly earnings	Total employed	Median weekly earnings	Total employed	Median weekly earnings	
Engineers, all other............................	315	$1,439	40	([1])	275	$1,456	([2])
Drafters...	129	962	21	([1])	108	958	([2])
Engineering technicians, except drafters..........	360	989	48	([1])	312	1,008	([2])
Surveying and mapping technicians..............	67	885	4	([1])	63	891	([2])
Life, physical, and social science occupations............	1,098	1,134	467	$1,015	631	1,226	82.8
Agricultural and food scientists..................	34	([1])	10	([1])	23	([1])	([2])
Biological scientists...............................	94	1,181	43	([1])	51	1,331	([2])
Conservation scientists and foresters..........	18	([1])	2	([1])	15	([1])	([2])
Medical scientists..................................	123	1,163	59	1,060	64	1,331	79.6
Astronomers and physicists......................	22	([1])	3	([1])	19	([1])	([2])
Atmospheric and space scientists..............	14	([1])	2	([1])	13	([1])	([2])
Chemists and materials scientists..............	98	1,163	42	([1])	56	1,226	([2])
Environmental scientists and geoscientists..........	93	1,266	25	([1])	68	1,390	([2])
Physical scientists, all other.....................	145	1,456	50	1,171	96	1,522	76.9
Economists..	23	([1])	5	([1])	18	([1])	([2])
Survey researchers................................	3	([1])	2	([1])	1	([1])	([2])
Psychologists.......................................	93	1,228	72	1,155	21	([1])	([2])
Sociologists...	4	([1])	1	([1])	2	([1])	([2])
Urban and regional planners.....................	28	([1])	12	([1])	16	([1])	([2])
Miscellaneous social scientists and related workers...........	44	([1])	22	([1])	22	([1])	([2])
Agricultural and food science technicians..........	29	([1])	15	([1])	14	([1])	([2])
Biological technicians.............................	14	([1])	6	([1])	8	([1])	([2])
Chemical technicians..............................	62	779	17	([1])	45	([1])	([2])
Geological and petroleum technicians..........	22	([1])	10	([1])	12	([1])	([2])
Nuclear technicians...............................	4	([1])	0	([1])	4	([1])	([2])
Social science research assistants..............	3	([1])	3	([1])	0	([1])	([2])
Miscellaneous life, physical, and social science technicians...........	128	745	66	620	62	825	75.2
Community and social services occupations....................	1,891	838	1,177	820	714	869	94.4
Counselors..	519	848	347	855	172	833	102.6
Social workers......................................	668	847	535	845	134	856	98.7
Probation officers and correctional treatment specialists...........	85	948	40	([1])	44	([1])	([2])
Social and human service assistants..........	124	637	99	656	25	([1])	([2])
Miscellaneous community and social service specialists, including health educators and community health workers...........	74	667	51	642	24	([1])	([2])
Clergy...	344	895	63	777	281	959	81.0
Directors, religious activities and education..........	37	([1])	23	([1])	14	([1])	([2])
Religious workers, all other......................	40	([1])	20	([1])	21	([1])	([2])
Legal occupations.....................................	1,315	1,328	716	1,013	600	1,884	53.8
Lawyers..	690	1,909	228	1,636	462	2,055	79.6
Judicial law clerks.................................	9	([1])	5	([1])	4	([1])	([2])
Judges, magistrates, and other judicial workers..............	64	1,637	26	([1])	38	([1])	([2])
Paralegals and legal assistants.................	372	872	317	865	54	919	94.1
Miscellaneous legal support workers..........	181	815	139	754	42	([1])	([2])
Education, training, and library occupations....................	6,454	915	4,687	858	1,766	1,133	75.7
Postsecondary teachers..........................	920	1,216	424	1,055	497	1,366	77.2
Preschool and kindergarten teachers..........	494	589	485	588	9	([1])	([2])
Elementary and middle school teachers..........	2,435	942	1,971	921	464	1,128	81.6
Secondary school teachers......................	1,043	1,009	578	978	465	1,050	93.1
Special education teachers......................	307	944	264	940	43	([1])	([2])

See footnotes at end of table.

Table 18. **Median usual weekly earnings of full-time wage and salary workers by detailed occupation and gender,** 2012 annual averages (continued)

Occupation	Both sexes		Women		Men		Women's earnings as a percentage of men's
	Number of workers (thousands)	Median weekly earnings	Total employed	Median weekly earnings	Total employed	Median weekly earnings	
Other teachers and instructors...................	372	$785	220	$729	151	$917	79.5
Archivists, curators, and museum technicians...............	40	([1])	21	([1])	20	([1])	([2])
Librarians..............................	143	966	120	960	24	([1])	([2])
Library technicians..............................	21	([1])	17	([1])	4	([1])	([2])
Teacher assistants..............................	567	458	515	452	51	493	91.7
Other education, training, and library workers...............	110	1,011	72	932	38	([1])	([2])
Arts, design, entertainment, sports, and media occupations..............................	1,440	969	631	885	809	1,055	83.9
Artists and related workers..............................	68	1,131	24	([1])	44	([1])	([2])
Designers..............................	467	953	226	855	241	1,028	83.2
Actors..............................	10	([1])	5	([1])	5	([1])	([2])
Producers and directors..............................	75	1,048	34	([1])	41	([1])	([2])
Athletes, coaches, umpires, and related workers.............	89	958	25	([1])	63	1,018	([2])
Dancers and choreographers..............................	5	([1])	5	([1])	0	([1])	([2])
Musicians, singers, and related workers..............	49	([1])	13	([1])	36	([1])	([2])
Entertainers and performers, sports and related workers, all other..............................	14	([1])	5	([1])	9	([1])	([2])
Announcers..............................	20	([1])	3	([1])	17	([1])	([2])
News analysts, reporters and correspondents...............	63	1,021	24	([1])	39	([1])	([2])
Public relations specialists..............................	133	1,127	79	989	55	1,351	73.2
Editors..............................	121	946	62	889	59	993	89.5
Technical writers..............................	52	1,227	27	([1])	24	([1])	([2])
Writers and authors..............................	86	899	46	([1])	40	([1])	([2])
Miscellaneous media and communication workers............	43	([1])	28	([1])	15	([1])	([2])
Broadcast and sound engineering technicians and radio operators..............................	70	875	5	([1])	64	924	([2])
Photographers..............................	37	([1])	14	([1])	24	([1])	([2])
Television, video, and motion picture camera operators and editors..............................	34	([1])	5	([1])	29	([1])	([2])
Media and communication equipment workers, all others..............................	3	([1])	2	([1])	1	([1])	([2])
Healthcare practitioners and technical occupations............	5,791	1,028	4,320	980	1,471	1,245	78.7
Chiropractors..............................	7	([1])	3	([1])	4	([1])	([2])
Dentists..............................	49	([1])	13	([1])	37	([1])	([2])
Dietitians and nutritionists..............................	79	840	73	845	6	([1])	([2])
Optometrists..............................	7	([1])	3	([1])	4	([1])	([2])
Pharmacists..............................	223	1,877	116	1,871	107	1,879	99.6
Physicians and surgeons..............................	655	1,887	226	1,418	429	2,099	67.6
Physician assistants..............................	88	1,329	61	1,364	27	([1])	([2])
Podiatrists..............................	1	([1])	1	([1])	0	([1])	([2])
Audiologists..............................	7	([1])	6	([1])	1	([1])	([2])
Occupational therapists..............................	85	1,189	82	1,200	3	([1])	([2])
Physical therapists..............................	144	1,287	88	1,190	56	1,362	87.4
Radiation therapists..............................	11	([1])	9	([1])	1	([1])	([2])
Recreational therapists..............................	10	([1])	9	([1])	1	([1])	([2])
Respiratory therapists..............................	92	979	56	936	36	([1])	([2])
Speech-language pathologists..............................	88	1,128	86	1,121	3	([1])	([2])
Exercise physiologists..............................	0	([1])	0	([1])	0	([1])	([2])
Therapists, all other..............................	88	926	71	877	16	([1])	([2])
Veterinarians..............................	49	([1])	29	([1])	20	([1])	([2])
Registered Nurses..............................	2,176	1,097	1,946	1,086	230	1,189	91.3
Nurse anesthetists..............................	24	([1])	12	([1])	11	([1])	([2])
Nurse midwives..............................	2	([1])	2	([1])	0	([1])	([2])
Nurse practitioners..............................	77	1,610	65	1,530	12	([1])	([2])

See footnotes at end of table.

Table 18. **Median usual weekly earnings of full-time wage and salary workers by detailed occupation and gender, 2012 annual averages (continued)**

Occupation	Both sexes		Women		Men		Women's earnings as a percentage of men's
	Number of workers (thousands)	Median weekly earnings	Total employed	Median weekly earnings	Total employed	Median weekly earnings	
Health diagnosing and treating practitioners, all other..............	3	(¹)	0	(¹)	3	(¹)	(²)
Clinical laboratory technologists and technicians...........	256	$869	180	$842	76	$943	89.3
Dental hygienists.........	51	1,045	50	1,047	0	(¹)	(²)
Diagnostic related technologists and technicians...........	241	961	174	912	67	1,131	80.6
Emergency medical technicians and paramedics...........	145	780	44	(¹)	100	809	(²)
Health practitioner support technologists and technicians.	403	615	322	621	82	599	103.7
Licensed practical and licensed vocational nurses..........	433	731	400	730	33	(¹)	(²)
Medical records and health information technicians..........	74	618	65	663	9	(¹)	(²)
Opticians, dispensing..........	41	(¹)	24	(¹)	17	(¹)	(²)
Miscellaneous health technologists and technicians..........	113	772	71	714	42	(¹)	(²)
Other healthcare practitioners and technical occupations..........	69	900	34	(¹)	36	(¹)	(²)
Service occupations..........	14,839	485	7,328	435	7,511	543	80.1
Health care support occupations..........	2,350	482	2,060	477	290	529	90.2
Nursing, psychiatric, and home health aides..........	1,458	451	1,285	445	173	508	87.6
Occupational therapy assistants and aides..........	11	(¹)	11	(¹)	0	(¹)	(²)
Physical therapist assistants and aides..........	45	(¹)	26	(¹)	19	(¹)	(²)
Massage therapists..........	42	(¹)	32	(¹)	11	(¹)	(²)
Dental assistants..........	174	579	172	581	2	(¹)	(²)
Medical assistants..........	323	514	302	515	21	(¹)	(²)
Medical transcriptionists..........	30	(¹)	29	(¹)	1	(¹)	(²)
Pharmacy aides..........	30	(¹)	28	(¹)	2	(¹)	(²)
Veterinary assistants and laboratory animal caretakers..........	22	(¹)	15	(¹)	7	(¹)	(²)
Phlebotomists..........	101	520	82	516	19	(¹)	(²)
Miscellaneous healthcare support occupations, including medical equipment preparers..........	112	487	77	462	35	(¹)	(²)
Protective service occupations..........	2,655	791	500	658	2,154	841	78.2
First-line supervisors of correctional officers..........	51	820	17	(¹)	33	(¹)	(²)
First-line supervisors of police and detectives..........	105	1,216	16	(¹)	89	1,240	(²)
First-line supervisors of fire fighting and prevention workers..........	59	1,271	0	(¹)	59	1,272	(²)
First-line supervisors, protective service workers, all other..........	80	881	26	(¹)	54	806	(²)
Firefighters..........	276	1,068	8	(¹)	268	1,073	(²)
Fire inspectors..........	15	(¹)	2	(¹)	13	(¹)	(²)
Bailiffs, correctional officers, and jailers..........	363	722	102	643	261	768	83.7
Detectives and criminal investigators..........	151	1,062	37	(¹)	114	1,171	(²)
Fish and game wardens..........	5	(¹)	1	(¹)	4	(¹)	(²)
Parking enforcement workers..........	3	(¹)	1	(¹)	2	(¹)	(²)
Police and sheriff's patrol officers..........	629	979	76	815	554	1,016	80.2
Transit and railroad police..........	3	(¹)	0	(¹)	3	(¹)	(²)
Animal control workers..........	8	(¹)	3	(¹)	5	(¹)	(²)
Private detectives and investigators..........	76	848	34	(¹)	42	(¹)	(²)
Security guards and gaming surveillance officers..........	742	528	138	501	603	537	93.3
Crossing guards..........	17	(¹)	9	(¹)	8	(¹)	(²)
Transportation security screeners..........	18	(¹)	6	(¹)	12	(¹)	(²)
Lifeguards and other recreational, and all other protective service workers..........	55	472	24	(¹)	32	(¹)	(²)

See footnotes at end of table.

Table 18. **Median usual weekly earnings of full-time wage and salary workers by detailed occupation and gender,**
2012 annual averages (continued)

Occupation	Both sexes		Women		Men		Women's earnings as a percentage of men's
	Number of workers (thousands)	Median weekly earnings	Total employed	Median weekly earnings	Total employed	Median weekly earnings	
Food preparation and serving related occupations............	4,164	$410	1,975	$389	2,189	$433	89.8
Chefs and head cooks...	318	562	56	462	261	582	79.4
First-line supervisors of food preparation and serving workers..	415	491	245	451	170	561	80.4
Cooks..	1,240	389	408	361	833	403	89.6
Food preparation workers...................................	432	383	241	357	191	408	87.5
Bartenders..	209	460	112	421	97	520	81.0
Combined food preparation and serving workers, including fast food..	166	382	109	368	57	406	90.6
Counter attendants, cafeteria, food concession, and coffee shop...	56	350	40	(^{1})	17	(^{1})	(^{2})
Waiters and waitresses......................................	891	411	569	396	322	456	86.8
Food servers, nonrestaurant................................	112	456	63	434	49	(^{1})	(^{2})
Dining room and cafeteria attendants and bartender helpers..	137	370	67	366	70	374	97.9
Dishwashers...	127	345	21	(^{1})	106	337	(^{2})
Hosts and hostesses, restaurant, lounge, and coffee shop...	59	391	44	(^{1})	15	(^{1})	(^{2})
Food preparation and serving related workers, all other..	1	(^{1})	0	(^{1})	1	(^{1})	(^{2})
Building and grounds cleaning and maintenance occupations...	3,430	465	1,156	407	2,275	501	81.2
First-line supervisors of housekeeping and janitorial workers...	159	569	72	505	88	687	73.5
First-line supervisors of landscaping, lawn service, and groundskeeping workers...........................	109	745	4	(^{1})	105	748	(^{2})
Janitors and building cleaners..............................	1,514	484	380	408	1,134	511	79.8
Maids and housekeeping cleaners..........................	791	399	668	395	123	425	92.9
Pest control workers...	62	571	3	(^{1})	59	570	(^{2})
Grounds maintenance workers..............................	795	455	29	(^{1})	766	452	(^{2})
Personal care and service occupations........................	2,241	468	1,637	428	603	569	75.2
First-line supervisors of gaming workers..................	92	752	34	(^{1})	59	864	(^{2})
First-line supervisors of personal service workers..	83	600	53	518	30	(^{1})	(^{2})
Animal trainers..	11	(^{1})	8	(^{1})	4	(^{1})	(^{2})
Nonfarm animal caretakers.................................	78	414	57	417	21	(^{1})	(^{2})
Gaming services workers....................................	74	604	38	(^{1})	36	(^{1})	(^{2})
Motion picture projectionists...............................	0	(^{1})	0	(^{1})	0	(^{1})	(^{2})
Ushers, lobby attendants, and ticket takers................	10	(^{1})	5	(^{1})	5	(^{1})	(^{2})
Miscellaneous entertainment attendants and related workers..	61	470	26	(^{1})	35	(^{1})	(^{2})
Embalmers and funeral attendants.........................	8	(^{1})	2	(^{1})	6	(^{1})	(^{2})
Morticians, undertakers, and funeral directors.............	23	(^{1})	3	(^{1})	19	(^{1})	(^{2})
Barbers...	57	466	15	(^{1})	42	(^{1})	(^{2})
Hairdressers, hairstylists, and cosmetologists.............	294	473	272	468	22	(^{1})	(^{2})
Miscellaneous personal appearance workers...............	154	427	123	430	31	(^{1})	(^{2})
Baggage porters, bellhops, and concierges................	49	(^{1})	7	(^{1})	41	(^{1})	(^{2})
Tour and travel guides......................................	20	(^{1})	8	(^{1})	12	(^{1})	(^{2})
Childcare workers...	425	390	395	386	31	(^{1})	(^{2})
Personal care aides...	549	422	450	412	99	465	88.6
Recreation and fitness workers.............................	174	575	102	542	71	675	80.3
Residential advisors...	48	(^{1})	27	(^{1})	21	(^{1})	(^{2})
Personal care and service workers, all other...............	32	(^{1})	13	(^{1})	19	(^{1})	(^{2})
Sales and office occupations....................................	23,115	655	13,914	610	9,202	768	79.4
Sales and related occupations.................................	9,433	689	4,005	521	5,428	838	62.2
First-line supervisors of retail sales workers..	2,295	711	977	598	1,317	792	75.5
First-line supervisors of non-retail sales workers..	791	1,045	220	847	571	1,130	75.0

See footnotes at end of table.

Table 18. **Median usual weekly earnings of full-time wage and salary workers by detailed occupation and gender,** 2012 annual averages (continued)

Occupation	Both sexes		Women		Men		Women's earnings as a percentage of men's
	Number of workers (thousands)	Median weekly earnings	Total employed	Median weekly earnings	Total employed	Median weekly earnings	
Cashiers..........	1,348	$376	941	$368	407	$400	92.0
Counter and rental clerks..........	96	495	42	([1])	54	591	([2])
Parts salespersons..........	88	643	9	([1])	79	661	([2])
Retail salespersons..........	1,842	576	707	436	1,135	678	64.3
Advertising sales agents..........	191	909	91	842	100	945	89.1
Insurance sales agents..........	389	827	191	641	197	1,026	62.5
Securities, commodities, and financial services sales agents..........	220	1,131	64	862	156	1,247	69.1
Travel agents..........	44	([1])	33	([1])	11	([1])	([2])
Sales representatives, services, all other..........	415	935	130	825	286	992	83.2
Sales representatives, wholesale and manufacturing..........	1,091	1,064	285	822	806	1,161	70.8
Models, demonstrators, and product promoters..........	18	([1])	12	([1])	6	([1])	([2])
Real estate brokers and sales agents..........	328	789	194	680	134	1,031	66.0
Sales engineers..........	26	([1])	1	([1])	25	([1])	([2])
Telemarketers..........	65	464	29	([1])	35	([1])	([2])
Door-to-door sales workers, news and street vendors, and related workers..........	43	([1])	16	([1])	27	([1])	([2])
Sales and related workers, all other..........	144	785	62	653	81	996	65.6
Office and administrative support occupations..........	13,683	643	9,909	629	3,774	700	89.9
First-line supervisors of office and administrative support workers..........	1,274	795	858	760	416	895	84.9
Switchboard operators, including answering service..........	28	([1])	20	([1])	8	([1])	([2])
Telephone operators..........	35	([1])	30	([1])	5	([1])	([2])
Communications equipment operators, all other..........	8	([1])	4	([1])	4	([1])	([2])
Bill and account collectors..........	183	640	122	633	61	681	93.0
Billing and posting clerks	394	627	347	615	47	([1])	([2])
Bookkeeping, accounting, and auditing clerks..........	857	677	755	672	102	740	90.8
Gaming cage workers..........	6	([1])	5	([1])	2	([1])	([2])
Payroll and timekeeping clerks..........	126	702	116	707	9	([1])	([2])
Procurement clerks..........	26	([1])	11	([1])	15	([1])	([2])
Tellers..........	268	497	238	499	30	([1])	([2])
Financial clerks, all other..........	44	([1])	32	([1])	12	([1])	([2])
Brokerage clerks..........	5	([1])	1	([1])	4	([1])	([2])
Correspondence clerks..........	6	([1])	4	([1])	2	([1])	([2])
Court, municipal, and license clerks..........	77	699	63	693	14	([1])	([2])
Credit authorizers, checkers, and clerks..........	42	([1])	31	([1])	10	([1])	([2])
Customer service representatives..........	1,535	608	1,033	585	502	684	85.5
Eligibility interviewers, government programs..........	78	769	61	730	17	([1])	([2])
File clerks..........	204	645	159	635	44	([1])	([2])
Hotel, motel, and resort desk clerks..........	73	522	44	([1])	29	([1])	([2])
Interviewers, except eligibility and loan..........	104	593	91	581	13	([1])	([2])
Library assistants, clerical..........	34	([1])	28	([1])	6	([1])	([2])
Loan interviewers and clerks..........	133	692	107	682	26	([1])	([2])
New accounts clerks..........	22	([1])	15	([1])	7	([1])	([2])
Order clerks..........	90	561	53	595	37	([1])	([2])
Human resources assistants, except payroll and timekeeping..........	105	759	88	724	17	([1])	([2])
Receptionists and information clerks..........	831	531	758	524	73	604	86.8
Reservation and transportation ticket agents and travel clerks..........	99	738	54	634	45	([1])	([2])
Information and record clerks, all other..........	87	661	73	677	15	([1])	([2])

See footnotes at end of table.

Table 18. **Median usual weekly earnings of full-time wage and salary workers by detailed occupation and gender,** 2012 annual averages (continued)

Occupation	Both sexes		Women		Men		Women's earnings as a percentage of men's
	Number of workers (thousands)	Median weekly earnings	Total employed	Median weekly earnings	Total employed	Median weekly earnings	
Cargo and freight agents...	21	([1])	5	([1])	15	([1])	([2])
Couriers and messengers...	139	$737	19	([1])	120	$744	([2])
Dispatchers...	252	648	159	$605	94	796	76.0
Meter readers, utilities...	25	([1])	5	([1])	21	([1])	([2])
Postal service clerks...	137	980	73	910	64	1,000	91.0
Postal service mail carriers...	279	990	93	907	186	1,026	88.4
Postal service mail sorters, processors, and processing machine operators...	56	891	23	([1])	33	([1])	([2])
Production, planning, and expediting clerks...	242	858	131	765	111	946	80.9
Shipping, receiving, and traffic clerks...	458	556	125	522	333	577	90.5
Stock clerks and order fillers...	936	505	310	484	625	516	93.8
Weighers, measurers, checkers, and samplers, recordkeeping...	64	638	29	([1])	35	([1])	([2])
Secretaries and administrative assistants...	2,251	669	2,146	665	105	803	82.8
Computer operators...	87	785	45	([1])	42	([1])	([2])
Data entry keyers...	259	591	202	586	57	611	95.9
Word processors and typists...	90	624	82	622	8	([1])	([2])
Desktop publishers...	3	([1])	0	([1])	3	([1])	([2])
Insurance claims and policy processing clerks...	226	643	182	631	44	([1])	([2])
Mail clerks and mail machine operators, except postal service...	72	580	27	([1])	44	([1])	([2])
Office clerks, general...	798	601	667	600	131	607	98.8
Office machine operators, except computer...	34	([1])	16	([1])	18	([1])	([2])
Proofreaders and copy markers...	5	([1])	4	([1])	1	([1])	([2])
Statistical assistants...	25	([1])	14	([1])	11	([1])	([2])
Office and administrative support workers, all other...	452	707	349	686	103	788	87.1
Natural resources, construction, and maintenance occupations...	9,968	740	389	550	9,579	749	73.4
Farming, fishing, and forestry occupations...	777	435	166	377	611	457	82.5
First-line supervisors of farming, fishing, and forestry workers...	39	([1])	5	([1])	34	([1])	([2])
Agricultural inspectors...	17	([1])	5	([1])	12	([1])	([2])
Animal breeders...	1	([1])	0	([1])	1	([1])	([2])
Graders and sorters, agricultural products...	108	410	70	396	37	([1])	([2])
Miscellaneous agricultural workers...	560	426	81	350	478	444	78.8
Fishers and related fishing workers...	8	([1])	1	([1])	8	([1])	([2])
Hunters and trappers...	2	([1])	2	([1])	0	([1])	([2])
Forest and conservation workers...	5	([1])	0	([1])	5	([1])	([2])
Logging workers...	37	([1])	2	([1])	36	([1])	([2])
Construction and extraction occupations...	5,102	740	98	723	5,004	741	97.6
First-line supervisors of construction trades and extraction workers...	488	1,019	13	([1])	475	1,018	([2])
Boilermakers...	23	([1])	0	([1])	23	([1])	([2])
Brickmasons, blockmasons, and stonemasons...	94	641	0	([1])	94	641	([2])
Carpenters...	750	675	7	([1])	743	673	([2])
Carpet, floor, and tile installers and finishers...	84	599	1	([1])	83	603	([2])
Cement masons, concrete finishers, and terrazzo workers...	53	601	0	([1])	53	601	([2])
Construction laborers...	937	607	24	([1])	913	609	([2])
Paving, surfacing, and tamping equipment operators...	15	([1])	0	([1])	15	([1])	([2])

See footnotes at end of table.

Table 18. **Median usual weekly earnings of full-time wage and salary workers by detailed occupation and gender, 2012 annual averages (continued)**

Occupation	Both sexes		Women		Men		Women's earnings as a percentage of men's
	Number of workers (thousands)	Median weekly earnings	Total employed	Median weekly earnings	Total employed	Median weekly earnings	
Pile-driver operators...............................	2	([1])	0	([1])	2	([1])	([2])
Operating engineers and other construction equipment operators...............................	321	$805	5	([1])	316	$805	([2])
Drywall installers, ceiling tile installers, and tapers...........	94	568	0	([1])	94	567	([2])
Electricians...	574	932	11	([1])	563	929	([2])
Glaziers...	38	([1])	0	([1])	38	([1])	([2])
Insulation workers......................................	33	([1])	0	([1])	32	([1])	([2])
Painters, construction and maintenance...................	261	568	8	([1])	252	559	([2])
Paperhangers...	2	([1])	0	([1])	2	([1])	([2])
Pipelayers, plumbers, pipefitters, and steamfitters...........	436	878	6	([1])	430	876	([2])
Plasterers and stucco masons.........................	14	([1])	0	([1])	14	([1])	([2])
Reinforcing iron and rebar workers....................	8	([1])	0	([1])	8	([1])	([2])
Roofers...	123	533	2	([1])	121	524	([2])
Sheet metal workers....................................	103	885	3	([1])	100	880	([2])
Structural iron and steel workers.....................	60	759	1	([1])	59	767	([2])
Solar photovoltaic installers...........................	4	([1])	0	([1])	4	([1])	([2])
Helpers, construction trades...........................	42	([1])	1	([1])	40	([1])	([2])
Construction and building inspectors...................	87	932	4	([1])	83	940	([2])
Elevator installers and repairers......................	31	([1])	1	([1])	29	([1])	([2])
Fence erectors...	26	([1])	0	([1])	26	([1])	([2])
Hazardous materials removal workers..................	28	([1])	4	([1])	23	([1])	([2])
Highway maintenance workers.........................	98	683	1	([1])	97	683	([2])
Rail-track laying and maintenance equipment operators...	7	([1])	0	([1])	7	([1])	([2])
Septic tank servicers and sewer pipe cleaners..............	6	([1])	0	([1])	6	([1])	([2])
Miscellaneous construction and related workers..............	24	([1])	1	([1])	23	([1])	([2])
Derrick, rotary drill, and service unit operators, oil, gas, and mining..................	32	([1])	1	([1])	32	([1])	([2])
Earth drillers, except oil and gas.....................	28	([1])	0	([1])	28	([1])	([2])
Explosives workers, ordnance handling experts, and blasters.........................	5	([1])	0	([1])	5	([1])	([2])
Mining machine operators..............................	65	997	0	([1])	65	996	([2])
Roof bolters, mining.....................................	4	([1])	0	([1])	4	([1])	([2])
Roustabouts, oil and gas...............................	16	([1])	1	([1])	15	([1])	([2])
Helpers—extraction workers...........................	3	([1])	0	([1])	3	([1])	([2])
Other extraction workers...............................	84	985	1	([1])	83	981	([2])
Installation, maintenance, and repair occupations.............	4,088	808	125	$757	3,963	809	93.6
First-line supervisors of mechanics, installers, and repairers....................	280	936	17	([1])	262	934	([2])
Computer, automated teller, and office machine repairers..........................	218	854	26	([1])	193	880	([2])
Radio and telecommunications equipment installers and repairers.................	142	885	10	([1])	132	898	([2])
Avionics technicians.....................................	10	([1])	3	([1])	7	([1])	([2])
Electric motor, power tool, and related repairers.............	37	([1])	0	([1])	37	([1])	([2])
Electrical and electronics installers and repairers, transportation equipment................	5	([1])	0	([1])	5	([1])	([2])
Electrical and electronics repairers, industrial and utility................	10	([1])	0	([1])	10	([1])	([2])
Electronic equipment installers and repairers, motor vehicles................	15	([1])	1	([1])	14	([1])	([2])
Electronic home entertainment equipment installers and repairers................	44	([1])	0	([1])	44	([1])	([2])

See footnotes at end of table.

Table 18. **Median usual weekly earnings of full-time wage and salary workers by detailed occupation and gender,** **2012 annual averages (continued)**

Occupation	Both sexes		Women		Men		Women's earnings as a percentage of men's
	Number of workers (thousands)	Median weekly earnings	Total employed	Median weekly earnings	Total employed	Median weekly earnings	
Security and fire alarm systems installers........................	34	([1])	0	([1])	34	([1])	([2])
Aircraft mechanics and service technicians....................	144	$993	2	([1])	142	$986	([2])
Automotive body and related repairers..........................	120	619	2	([1])	119	618	([2])
Automotive glass installers and repairers......................	17	([1])	0	([1])	17	([1])	([2])
Automotive service technicians and mechanics..............	691	702	7	([1])	684	704	([2])
Bus and truck mechanics and diesel engine specialists...	271	843	1	([1])	271	844	([2])
Heavy vehicle and mobile equipment service technicians and mechanics.......................................	174	941	3	([1])	171	942	([2])
Small engine mechanics..	42	([1])	1	([1])	41	([1])	([2])
Miscellaneous vehicle and mobile equipment mechanics, installers, and repairers........................	67	493	1	([1])	66	496	([2])
Control and valve installers and repairers.....................	25	([1])	1	([1])	24	([1])	([2])
Heating, air conditioning, and refrigeration mechanics and installers.......................................	280	827	4	([1])	276	829	([2])
Home appliance repairers..	35	([1])	3	([1])	33	([1])	([2])
Industrial and refractory machinery mechanics..............	424	867	10	([1])	415	871	([2])
Maintenance and repair workers, general.....................	371	731	6	([1])	364	732	([2])
Maintenance workers, machinery..................................	25	([1])	3	([1])	22	([1])	([2])
Millwrights...	50	938	3	([1])	46	([1])	([2])
Electrical power-line installers and repairers.................	117	988	2	([1])	115	990	([2])
Telecommunications line installers and repairers............	171	915	8	([1])	164	910	([2])
Precision instrument and equipment repairers................	44	([1])	5	([1])	38	([1])	([2])
Wind turbine service technicians.................................	1	([1])	0	([1])	1	([1])	([2])
Coin, vending, and amusement machine servicers and repairers..	23	([1])	1	([1])	22	([1])	([2])
Commercial divers..	0	([1])	0	([1])	0	([1])	([2])
Locksmiths and safe repairers....................................	17	([1])	0	([1])	17	([1])	([2])
Manufactured building and mobile home installers...........	4	([1])	0	([1])	4	([1])	([2])
Riggers..	10	([1])	0	([1])	10	([1])	([2])
Signal and track switch repairers................................	3	([1])	0	([1])	3	([1])	([2])
Helpers—installation, maintenance, and repair workers..	20	([1])	0	([1])	20	([1])	([2])
Other installation, maintenance, and repair workers..	147	677	5	([1])	142	671	([2])
Production, transportation, and material moving occupations..	13,842	624	2,773	$493	11,069	675	73.0
Production occupations..	7,427	627	1,930	496	5,497	695	71.4
First-line supervisors of production and operating workers..	734	917	132	674	601	954	70.6
Aircraft structure, surfaces, rigging, and systems assemblers..	22	([1])	5	([1])	17	([1])	([2])
Electrical, electronics, and electromechanical assemblers..	155	564	78	520	77	620	83.9
Engine and other machine assemblers..........................	32	([1])	5	([1])	26	([1])	([2])
Structural metal fabricators and fitters.........................	19	([1])	2	([1])	17	([1])	([2])
Miscellaneous assemblers and fabricators....................	833	557	320	499	513	606	82.3
Bakers...	121	474	55	450	65	501	89.8
Butchers and other meat, poultry, and fish processing workers...	273	507	64	417	208	537	77.7
Food and tobacco roasting, baking, and drying machine operators and tenders...............................	10	([1])	4	([1])	5	([1])	([2])

See footnotes at end of table.

Table 18. **Median usual weekly earnings of full-time wage and salary workers by detailed occupation and gender,** 2012 annual averages (continued)

Occupation	Both sexes		Women		Men		Women's earnings as a percentage of men's
	Number of workers (thousands)	Median weekly earnings	Total employed	Median weekly earnings	Total employed	Median weekly earnings	
Food batchmakers....................................	59	$512	32	([1])	27	([1])	([2])
Food cooking machine operators and tenders...............	13	([1])	4	([1])	9	([1])	([2])
Food processing workers, all other.......................	90	529	23	([1])	67	$549	([2])
Computer control programmers and operators...............	67	710	5	([1])	62	728	([2])
Extruding and drawing machine setters, operators, and tenders, metal and plastic....................	10	([1])	3	([1])	7	([1])	([2])
Forging machine setters, operators, and tenders, metal and plastic..........................	10	([1])	0	([1])	10	([1])	([2])
Rolling machine setters, operators, and tenders, metal and plastic..........................	7	([1])	0	([1])	7	([1])	([2])
Cutting, punching, and press machine setters, operators, and tenders, metal and plastic..........	80	556	15	([1])	65	575	([2])
Drilling and boring machine tool setters, operators, and tenders, metal and plastic..........	3	([1])	1	([1])	2	([1])	([2])
Grinding, lapping, polishing, and buffing machine tool setters, operators, and tenders, metal and plastic....................................	53	588	5	([1])	48	([1])	([2])
Lathe and turning machine tool setters, operators, and tenders, metal and plastic..............	15	([1])	4	([1])	11	([1])	([2])
Milling and planing machine setters, operators, and tenders, metal and plastic..............	3	([1])	0	([1])	3	([1])	([2])
Machinists..	381	760	16	([1])	366	762	([2])
Metal furnace operators, tenders, pourers, and casters.....	12	([1])	1	([1])	12	([1])	([2])
Model makers and patternmakers, metal and plastic..	7	([1])	1	([1])	6	([1])	([2])
Molders and molding machine setters, operators, and tenders, metal and plastic....................	38	([1])	9	([1])	30	([1])	([2])
Multiple machine tool setters, operators, and tenders, metal and plastic.........................	7	([1])	0	([1])	7	([1])	([2])
Tool and die makers....................................	51	1,005	0	([1])	51	1,005	([2])
Welding, soldering, and brazing workers.......................	551	712	26	([1])	525	722	([2])
Heat treating equipment setters, operators, and tenders, metal and plastic.........................	5	([1])	0	([1])	5	([1])	([2])
Layout workers, metal and plastic............................	6	([1])	0	([1])	6	([1])	([2])
Plating and coating machine setters, operators, and tenders, metal and plastic.......................	16	([1])	2	([1])	13	([1])	([2])
Tool grinders, filers, and sharpeners...........................	2	([1])	0	([1])	2	([1])	([2])
Metal workers and plastic workers, all other..................	374	618	70	$544	304	645	84.3
Prepress technicians and workers............................	23	([1])	9	([1])	14	([1])	([2])
Printing press operators....................................	167	628	28	([1])	139	666	([2])
Print binding and finishing workers...........................	17	([1])	9	([1])	8	([1])	([2])
Laundry and dry-cleaning workers...........................	123	410	66	359	57	462	77.7
Pressers, textile, garment, and related materials.............	41	([1])	29	([1])	12	([1])	([2])
Sewing machine operators.................................	127	385	86	369	41	([1])	([2])
Shoe and leather workers and repairers......................	5	([1])	2	([1])	3	([1])	([2])
Shoe machine operators and tenders........................	10	([1])	5	([1])	5	([1])	([2])
Tailors, dressmakers, and sewers...........................	42	([1])	30	([1])	12	([1])	([2])
Textile bleaching and dyeing machine operators and tenders....................................	5	([1])	1	([1])	5	([1])	([2])
Textile cutting machine setters, operators, and tenders..	9	([1])	4	([1])	5	([1])	([2])
Textile knitting and weaving machine setters, operators, and tenders................................	6	([1])	5	([1])	0	([1])	([2])

See footnotes at end of table.

Table 18. **Median usual weekly earnings of full-time wage and salary workers by detailed occupation and gender,** 2012 annual averages (continued)

Occupation	Both sexes		Women		Men		Women's earnings as a percentage of men's
	Number of workers (thousands)	Median weekly earnings	Total employed	Median weekly earnings	Total employed	Median weekly earnings	
Textile winding, twisting, and drawing out machine setters, operators, and tenders......	15	(1)	5	(1)	10	(1)	(2)
Extruding and forming machine setters, operators, and tenders, synthetic and glass fibers..........	2	(1)	0	(1)	2	(1)	(2)
Fabric and apparel patternmakers...............	1	(1)	1	(1)	0	(1)	(2)
Upholsterers...............	14	(1)	1	(1)	12	(1)	(2)
Textile, apparel, and furnishings workers, all other..........	16	(1)	10	(1)	6	(1)	(2)
Cabinetmakers and bench carpenters...............	35	(1)	2	(1)	34	(1)	(2)
Furniture finishers...............	5	(1)	2	(1)	3	(1)	(2)
Model makers and patternmakers, wood...............	0	(1)	0	(1)	0	(1)	(2)
Sawing machine setters, operators, and tenders, wood...............	26	(1)	1	(1)	25	(1)	(2)
Woodworking machine setters, operators, and tenders, except sawing...............	21	(1)	3	(1)	18	(1)	(2)
Woodworkers, all other...............	12	(1)	0	(1)	12	(1)	(2)
Power plant operators, distributors, and dispatchers...............	43	(1)	2	(1)	41	(1)	(2)
Stationary engineers and boiler operators...............	105	$830	6	(1)	99	$831	(2)
Water and wastewater treatment plant and system operators...............	70	862	3	(1)	67	870	(2)
Miscellaneous plant and system operators...............	35	(1)	4	(1)	31	(1)	(2)
Chemical processing machine setters, operators, and tenders...............	72	851	10	(1)	62	890	(2)
Crushing, grinding, polishing, mixing, and blending workers...............	86	628	12	(1)	74	651	(2)
Cutting workers...............	60	524	11	(1)	49	(1)	(2)
Extruding, forming, pressing, and compacting machine setters, operators, and tenders...............	38	(1)	10	(1)	28	(1)	(2)
Furnace, kiln, oven, drier, and kettle operators and tenders...............	14	(1)	1	(1)	12	(1)	(2)
Inspectors, testers, sorters, samplers, and weighers...............	621	729	206	$570	416	824	69.2
Jewelers and precious stone and metal workers...............	22	(1)	9	(1)	13	(1)	(2)
Medical, dental, and ophthalmic laboratory technicians...............	76	585	42	(1)	35	(1)	(2)
Packaging and filling machine operators and tenders...............	242	481	131	431	111	553	77.9
Painting workers...............	135	626	24	(1)	111	654	(2)
Photographic process workers and processing machine operators...............	39	(1)	15	(1)	24	(1)	(2)
Semiconductor processors...............	6	(1)	3	(1)	2	(1)	(2)
Adhesive bonding machine operators and tenders..........	8	(1)	2	(1)	6	(1)	(2)
Cleaning, washing, and metal pickling equipment operators and tenders...............	8	(1)	1	(1)	7	(1)	(2)
Cooling and freezing equipment operators and tenders...............	2	(1)	1	(1)	1	(1)	(2)
Etchers and engravers...............	4	(1)	1	(1)	3	(1)	(2)
Molders, shapers, and casters, except metal and plastic...............	26	(1)	5	(1)	21	(1)	(2)
Paper goods machine setters, operators, and tenders...............	32	(1)	9	(1)	23	(1)	(2)
Tire builders...............	17	(1)	3	(1)	14	(1)	(2)
Helpers—production workers...............	40	(1)	13	(1)	26	(1)	(2)

See footnotes at end of table.

Table 18. **Median usual weekly earnings of full-time wage and salary workers by detailed occupation and gender, 2012 annual averages (continued)**

Occupation	Both sexes		Women		Men		Women's earnings as a percentage of men's
	Number of workers (thousands)	Median weekly earnings	Total employed	Median weekly earnings	Total employed	Median weekly earnings	
Production workers, all other..........................	849	$584	223	$504	626	$619	81.4
Transportation and material moving occupations..............	6,415	621	843	487	5,572	650	74.9
Supervisors, transportation and material moving workers..........................	189	812	42	([1])	146	873	([2])
Aircraft pilots and flight engineers..........................	90	1,440	4	([1])	86	1,444	([2])
Air traffic controllers and airfield operations specialists..........................	47	([1])	3	([1])	44	([1])	([2])
Flight attendants..........................	59	775	42	([1])	16	([1])	([2])
Ambulance drivers and attendants, except emergency medical technicians..........................	16	([1])	3	([1])	13	([1])	([2])
Bus drivers..........................	302	601	126	516	177	652	79.1
Driver/sales workers and truck drivers..........................	2,533	730	101	537	2,433	736	73.0
Taxi drivers and chauffeurs..........................	183	554	22	([1])	161	572	([2])
Motor vehicle operators, all other..........................	35	([1])	7	([1])	28	([1])	([2])
Locomotive engineers and operators..........................	44	([1])	2	([1])	42	([1])	([2])
Railroad brake, signal, and switch operators..........................	9	([1])	0	([1])	9	([1])	([2])
Railroad conductors and yardmasters..........................	46	([1])	2	([1])	45	([1])	([2])
Subway, streetcar, and other rail transportation workers..........................	12	([1])	0	([1])	12	([1])	([2])
Sailors and marine oilers..........................	15	([1])	1	([1])	14	([1])	([2])
Ship and boat captains and operators..........................	29	([1])	1	([1])	28	([1])	([2])
Ship engineers..........................	5	([1])	0	([1])	5	([1])	([2])
Bridge and lock tenders..........................	8	([1])	0	([1])	8	([1])	([2])
Parking lot attendants..........................	50	404	5	([1])	45	([1])	([2])
Automotive and watercraft service attendants..........................	67	428	4	([1])	63	453	([2])
Transportation inspectors..........................	29	([1])	4	([1])	25	([1])	([2])
Transportation attendants, except flight attendants..........	23	([1])	15	([1])	8	([1])	([2])
Other transportation workers..........................	14	([1])	1	([1])	13	([1])	([2])
Conveyor operators and tenders..........................	3	([1])	2	([1])	1	([1])	([2])
Crane and tower operators..........................	61	753	3	([1])	58	777	([2])
Dredge, excavating, and loading machine operators..........................	32	([1])	1	([1])	31	([1])	([2])
Hoist and winch operators..........................	5	([1])	0	([1])	5	([1])	([2])
Industrial truck and tractor operators..........................	498	562	31	([1])	467	566	([2])
Cleaners of vehicles and equipment..........................	217	425	30	([1])	187	431	([2])
Laborers and freight, stock, and material movers, hand..........................	1,322	510	218	476	1,103	519	91.7
Machine feeders and offbearers..........................	26	([1])	8	([1])	18	([1])	([2])
Packers and packagers, hand..........................	306	404	160	394	146	426	92.5
Pumping station operators..........................	21	([1])	1	([1])	20	([1])	([2])
Refuse and recyclable material collectors..........................	75	501	3	([1])	71	497	([2])
Mine shuttle car operators..........................	1	([1])	0	([1])	1	([1])	([2])
Tank car, truck, and ship loaders..........................	3	([1])	0	([1])	3	([1])	([2])
Material moving workers, all other..........................	40	([1])	1	([1])	39	([1])	([2])

[1] Data not shown where the employment base is less than 50,000.

[2] Data not shown where the employment base for either the numerator or denominator is less than 50,000.

Source: Current Population Survey, U.S. Bureau of Labor Statistics.

Table 19. **Median usual weekly earnings of full-time wage and salary workers, by industry and gender, 2012 annual averages**

Industry	Total		Women		Men		Women's earnings as a percentage of men's
	Total employed	Median weekly earnings	Total employed	Median weekly earnings	Total employed	Median weekly earnings	
Total, 16 years and older.........................	102,749	$768	45,462	$691	57,286	$854	80.9
Agriculture and related industries	1,018	480	196	443	822	489	90.6
Mining, quarrying, and oil and gas extraction ...	899	1,112	112	922	787	1,146	80.5
Construction	5,967	772	482	760	5,485	774	98.2
Manufacturing	13,287	798	3,675	653	9,612	866	75.4
Durable goods	8,496	829	2,080	699	6,417	888	78.7
Nondurable goods	4,790	737	1,595	594	3,195	821	72.4
Wholesale and retail trade	13,310	631	5,198	544	8,112	715	76.1
Wholesale trade	3,088	823	851	715	2,237	872	82.0
Retail trade	10,222	593	4,347	515	5,875	660	78.0
Transportation and utilities	6,011	868	1,323	762	4,688	899	84.8
Transportation and warehousing	4,858	820	1,065	736	3,793	857	85.9
Utilities	1,153	1,036	259	885	894	1,105	80.1
Information	2,395	970	886	841	1,509	1,079	77.9
Financial activities	7,608	889	4,131	759	3,477	1,121	67.7
Finance and insurance	5,878	942	3,368	769	2,510	1,288	59.7
Real estate and rental and leasing	1,730	733	763	711	967	751	94.7
Professional and business services	11,299	912	4,451	783	6,848	1,013	77.3
Professional and technical services	7,012	1,166	2,915	939	4,097	1,389	67.6
Management, administrative, and waste services...	4,287	588	1,536	573	2,751	596	96.1
Education and health services	23,614	793	17,290	745	6,325	963	77.4
Educational services	9,722	885	6,567	840	3,155	997	84.3
Health care and social assistance	13,892	728	10,723	686	3,170	925	74.2
Leisure and hospitality	6,994	485	3,167	428	3,828	518	82.6
Arts, entertainment, and recreation	1,542	641	598	589	944	693	85.0
Accomodation and food services	5,452	447	2,568	408	2,884	486	84.0
Other services	4,088	622	1,781	518	2,308	722	71.7
Other services, except private households	3,743	649	1,476	558	2,267	725	77.0
Private households	346	410	305	406	41	(^{1})	(^{1})
Public administration....................................	6,258	928	2,770	820	3,488	1,041	78.8

[1] Data not shown where the employment base is less than 50,000.

Source: Current Population Survey, U.S. Bureau of Labor Statistics.

Table 20. **Employed persons, by full- and part-time status and gender, 1970–2012 annual averages**

(Numbers in thousands)

Year	Total				
	Total employed	Usually full time[1]	Usually part time[2]	Percentage usually full time	Percentage usually part time
1970	78,678	66,753	11,925	84.8	15.2
1971	79,367	66,973	12,393	84.4	15.6
1972	82,153	69,214	12,939	84.3	15.7
1973	85,064	71,803	13,262	84.4	15.6
1974	86,794	73,093	13,701	84.2	15.8
1975	85,846	71,586	14,260	83.4	16.6
1976	88,752	73,964	14,788	83.3	16.7
1977	92,017	76,625	15,391	83.3	16.7
1978	96,048	80,193	15,855	83.5	16.5
1979	98,824	82,654	16,171	83.6	16.4
1980	99,303	82,562	16,740	83.1	16.9
1981	100,397	83,243	17,154	82.9	17.1
1982	99,526	81,421	18,106	81.8	18.2
1983	100,834	82,322	18,511	81.6	18.4
1984	105,005	86,544	18,462	82.4	17.6
1985	107,150	88,534	18,615	82.6	17.4
1986	109,597	90,529	19,069	82.6	17.4
1987	112,440	92,957	19,483	82.7	17.3
1988	114,968	95,214	19,754	82.8	17.2
1989	117,342	97,369	19,973	83.0	17.0
1990	118,793	98,666	20,128	83.1	16.9
1991	117,718	97,190	20,528	82.6	17.4
1992	118,492	97,664	20,828	82.4	17.6
1993	120,259	99,114	21,145	82.4	17.6
1994	123,060	99,772	23,288	81.1	18.9
1995	124,900	101,679	23,220	81.4	18.6
1996	126,708	103,537	23,170	81.7	18.3
1997	129,558	106,334	23,224	82.1	17.9
1998	131,463	108,202	23,261	82.3	17.7
1999	133,488	110,302	23,186	82.6	17.4
2000	136,891	113,846	23,044	83.2	16.8
2001	136,933	113,573	23,361	82.9	17.1
2002	136,485	112,700	23,785	82.6	17.4
2003	137,736	113,324	24,412	82.3	17.7
2004	139,252	114,518	24,734	82.2	17.8
2005	141,730	117,016	24,714	82.6	17.4
2006	144,427	119,688	24,739	82.9	17.1
2007	146,047	121,091	24,956	82.9	17.1
2008	145,362	120,030	25,332	82.6	17.4
2009	139,877	112,634	27,244	80.5	19.5
2010	139,064	111,714	27,350	80.3	19.7
2011	139,869	112,556	27,313	80.5	19.5
2012	142,469	114,809	27,661	80.6	19.4

See footnotes at end of table.

Table 20. **Employed persons, by full- and part-time status and gender, 1970–2012 annual averages (continued)**

(Numbers in thousands)

Year	Women				
	Total employed	Usually full time[1]	Usually part time[2]	Percentage usually full time	Percentage usually part time
1970	29,688	21,929	7,758	73.9	26.1
1971	29,976	21,950	8,026	73.2	26.8
1972	31,257	22,842	8,416	73.1	26.9
1973	32,715	23,960	8,756	73.2	26.8
1974	33,769	24,714	9,055	73.2	26.8
1975	33,989	24,598	9,391	72.4	27.6
1976	35,615	25,814	9,799	72.5	27.5
1977	37,289	27,076	10,213	72.6	27.4
1978	39,569	28,912	10,658	73.1	26.9
1979	41,217	30,227	10,990	73.3	26.7
1980	42,117	30,845	11,270	73.2	26.8
1981	43,000	31,337	11,664	72.9	27.1
1982	43,256	31,086	12,170	71.9	28.1
1983	44,047	31,679	12,367	71.9	28.1
1984	45,915	33,473	12,441	72.9	27.1
1985	47,259	34,672	12,587	73.4	26.6
1986	48,706	35,845	12,862	73.6	26.4
1987	50,334	37,210	13,124	73.9	26.1
1988	51,696	38,398	13,298	74.3	25.7
1989	53,027	39,484	13,544	74.5	25.5
1990	53,689	40,165	13,524	74.8	25.2
1991	53,496	39,783	13,713	74.4	25.6
1992	54,052	40,301	13,751	74.6	25.4
1993	54,910	40,991	13,919	74.7	25.3
1994	56,610	40,940	15,670	72.3	27.7
1995	57,523	41,743	15,779	72.6	27.4
1996	58,501	42,776	15,725	73.1	26.9
1997	59,873	44,076	15,797	73.6	26.4
1998	60,771	45,014	15,757	74.1	25.9
1999	62,042	46,372	15,670	74.7	25.3
2000	63,586	47,916	15,670	75.4	24.6
2001	63,737	47,950	15,788	75.2	24.8
2002	63,582	47,494	16,088	74.7	25.3
2003	64,404	47,946	16,459	74.4	25.6
2004	64,728	48,073	16,654	74.3	25.7
2005	65,757	49,158	16,598	74.8	25.2
2006	66,925	50,380	16,545	75.3	24.7
2007	67,792	51,056	16,736	75.3	24.7
2008	67,876	51,178	16,698	75.4	24.6
2009	66,208	48,683	17,525	73.5	26.5
2010	65,705	48,214	17,491	73.4	26.6
2011	65,579	48,224	17,355	73.5	26.5
2012	66,914	49,331	17,583	73.7	26.3

See footnotes at end of table.

Table 20. **Employed persons, by full- and part-time status and gender, 1970–2012 annual averages (continued)**

(Numbers in thousands)

Year	Men				
	Total employed	Usually full time[1]	Usually part time[2]	Percentage usually full time	Percentage usually part time
1970	48,990	44,825	4,166	91.5	8.5
1971	49,390	45,023	4,367	91.2	8.8
1972	50,896	46,373	4,523	91.1	8.9
1973	52,349	47,843	4,507	91.4	8.6
1974	53,024	48,378	4,646	91.2	8.8
1975	51,857	46,988	4,870	90.6	9.4
1976	53,138	48,150	4,988	90.6	9.4
1977	54,728	49,551	5,178	90.5	9.5
1978	56,479	51,281	5,198	90.8	9.2
1979	57,607	52,427	5,180	91.0	9.0
1980	57,186	51,717	5,471	90.4	9.6
1981	57,397	51,906	5,492	90.4	9.6
1982	56,271	50,334	5,937	89.4	10.6
1983	56,787	50,643	6,145	89.2	10.8
1984	59,091	53,070	6,020	89.8	10.2
1985	59,891	53,862	6,028	89.9	10.1
1986	60,892	54,685	6,207	89.8	10.2
1987	62,107	55,746	6,360	89.8	10.2
1988	63,273	56,816	6,457	89.8	10.2
1989	64,315	57,885	6,430	90.0	10.0
1990	65,104	58,501	6,604	89.9	10.1
1991	64,223	57,407	6,815	89.4	10.6
1992	64,440	57,363	7,077	89.0	11.0
1993	65,349	58,123	7,226	88.9	11.1
1994	66,450	58,832	7,617	88.5	11.5
1995	67,377	59,936	7,441	89.0	11.0
1996	68,207	60,762	7,445	89.1	10.9
1997	69,685	62,258	7,427	89.3	10.7
1998	70,693	63,189	7,504	89.4	10.6
1999	71,446	63,930	7,516	89.5	10.5
2000	73,305	65,930	7,375	89.9	10.1
2001	73,196	65,623	7,573	89.7	10.3
2002	72,903	65,205	7,697	89.4	10.6
2003	73,332	65,379	7,953	89.2	10.8
2004	74,524	66,444	8,080	89.2	10.8
2005	75,973	67,858	8,115	89.3	10.7
2006	77,502	69,307	8,194	89.4	10.6
2007	78,254	70,035	8,220	89.5	10.5
2008	77,486	68,853	8,634	88.9	11.1
2009	73,670	63,951	9,719	86.8	13.2

See footnotes at end of table.

Table 20. **Employed persons, by full- and part-time status and gender, 1970–2012 annual averages (continued)**

(Numbers in thousands)

Year	Men				
	Total employed	Usually full time[1]	Usually part time[2]	Percentage usually full time	Percentage usually part time
2010	73,359	63,501	9,858	86.6	13.4
2011	74,290	64,333	9,957	86.6	13.4
2012	75,555	65,477	10,078	86.7	13.3

[1] Prior to 1994, total includes persons who usually work part time but who worked 35 or more hours during the reference week; for 1994 and later years, such persons were included in the part-time total. In all years, the total includes those who usually work full time but who worked less than 35 hours during the reference week for noneconomic reasons, such as illness or holiday, and those absent from work for the entire reference week who usually work full time. These groups are not shown separately.

[2] For all years, total includes those who usually work less than 35 hours a week but who were absent from work for the entire reference week, and for 1994 and later years, those who worked 35 or more hours during the reference week. These groups are not shown separately.

Note: Revisions to population controls and other changes can affect the comparability of labor force levels over time. In recent years, for example, updated population controls have been introduced annually with the release of January data. Information about historical comparability is online at www.bls.gov/cps/documentation.htm#comp.

Source: Current Population Survey, U.S. Bureau of Labor Statistics.

Table 21. **Average weekly hours at work in all industries and in nonagricultural industries, by gender, 1976–2012 annual averages**

Year	All industries			Nonagricultural industries		
	Total	Women	Men	Total	Women	Men
1976	38.7	34.1	41.7	38.4	34.1	41.4
1977	38.8	34.2	41.9	38.5	34.2	41.6
1978	39.0	34.5	42.1	38.7	34.4	41.8
1979	38.9	34.5	42.0	38.6	34.4	41.7
1980	38.5	34.5	41.5	38.3	34.4	41.2
1981	38.1	34.1	41.1	37.9	34.1	40.7
1982	38.0	34.1	40.9	37.7	34.0	40.6
1983	38.3	34.5	41.2	38.1	34.4	41.0
1984	38.8	34.9	41.8	38.6	34.9	41.5
1985	39.0	35.2	42.0	38.9	35.2	41.8
1986	39.1	35.4	42.1	38.9	35.3	41.9
1987	39.0	35.3	42.0	38.8	35.3	41.8
1988	39.4	35.7	42.4	39.3	35.7	42.2
1989	39.6	35.8	42.6	39.4	35.8	42.4
1990	39.4	35.8	42.3	39.3	35.8	42.1
1991	39.2	35.8	42.0	39.1	35.8	41.9
1992	38.9	35.6	41.7	38.8	35.6	41.6
1993	39.4	36.0	42.2	39.3	36.0	42.1
1994	39.2	35.5	42.2	39.1	35.6	42.1
1995	39.3	35.6	42.3	39.2	35.7	42.2
1996	39.3	35.7	42.3	39.2	35.7	42.2
1997	39.5	36.0	42.4	39.4	36.0	42.3
1998	39.3	35.8	42.2	39.2	35.9	42.2
1999	39.6	36.2	42.4	39.5	36.2	42.4
2000	39.7	36.4	42.5	39.6	36.4	42.4
2001	39.2	36.1	41.9	39.2	36.1	41.8
2002	39.2	36.0	41.8	39.1	36.1	41.7
2003	39.0	35.9	41.7	39.0	35.9	41.6
2004	39.0	35.9	41.7	39.0	35.9	41.6
2005	39.2	36.1	41.8	39.1	36.1	41.7
2006	39.2	36.2	41.8	39.2	36.2	41.7
2007	39.2	36.1	41.7	39.1	36.1	41.6
2008	38.9	36.1	41.3	38.8	36.1	41.2
2009	37.9	35.3	40.2	37.8	35.3	40.1
2010	38.2	35.5	40.5	38.1	35.6	40.4
2011	38.3	35.6	40.6	38.2	35.6	40.6
2012	38.5	35.8	40.8	38.4	35.8	40.7

Note: Revisions to population controls and other changes can affect the comparability of labor force levels over time. In recent years, for example, updated population controls have been introduced annually with the release of January data. Information about historical comparability is online at www.bls.gov/cps/documentation.htm#comp.

Source: Current Population Survey, U.S. Bureau of Labor Statistics.

Table 22. **Work experience of the population, by gender and full- and part-time status, selected years, 1970–2011**

(Percentage distribution)

	Population in thousands	With work experience			Percent distribution by work experience						
		Total in thousands	Percentage of population	Total	Usually work full time			Usually work part time			
					Total	50 to 52 weeks	1 to 49 weeks	Total	50 to 52 weeks	1 to 49 weeks	
Total											
1970............	138,953	93,850	67.5	100.0	79.4	55.6	23.8	20.6	6.7	13.9	
1975............	153,180	102,603	67.0	100.0	78.9	54.3	24.6	21.2	7.5	13.7	
1980............	169,452	115,752	68.3	100.0	78.5	56.1	22.4	21.4	7.7	13.7	
1985............	179,944	123,466	68.6	100.0	78.2	58.7	19.5	21.9	8.3	13.6	
1990	189,238	132,562	70.1	100.0	78.8	60.4	18.4	21.3	8.7	12.6	
1995............	199,925	138,971	69.5	100.0	78.6	62.9	15.7	21.3	9.1	12.2	
2000	214,292	150,787	70.4	100.0	80.4	66.7	13.7	19.5	9.3	10.2	
2005............	227,975	154,322	67.7	100.0	80.3	67.5	12.8	19.7	10.0	9.7	
2006............	231,033	156,658	67.8	100.0	80.9	68.4	12.5	19.1	9.7	9.4	
2007............	232,995	157,653	67.7	100.0	80.9	68.4	12.5	19.1	9.8	9.3	
2008............	235,086	157,472	67.0	100.0	79.5	65.6	13.9	20.5	10.5	10.0	
2009............	237,158	153,929	64.9	100.0	78.3	64.0	14.3	21.7	11.3	10.4	
2010............	238,999	158,882	66.5	100.0	78.2	64.7	13.6	21.8	11.2	10.5	
2011............	242,602	159,693	65.8	100.0	78.2	65.8	12.8	21.4	11.2	10.2	
Women											
1970............	73,657	38,809	52.7	100.0	67.9	40.7	27.2	32.2	10.1	22.1	
1975............	80,834	43,511	53.8	100.0	67.1	41.4	25.7	32.8	11.7	21.1	
1980............	89,259	51,492	57.7	100.0	67.7	44.7	23.0	32.3	11.9	20.4	
1985............	94,490	56,165	59.4	100.0	68.1	48.9	19.2	31.8	12.3	19.5	
1990	98,970	61,494	62.1	100.0	69.8	51.5	18.3	30.2	12.8	17.4	
1995............	104,058	65,304	62.8	100.0	70.2	54.3	15.9	29.7	13.3	16.4	
2000	111,440	71,341	64.0	100.0	72.9	58.4	14.5	27.1	13.4	13.7	
2005............	117,814	72,309	61.4	100.0	72.7	59.9	12.8	27.3	14.1	13.2	
2006............	119,300	73,527	61.6	100.0	73.0	60.7	12.3	27.0	14.1	12.9	
2007............	120,300	74,115	61.6	100.0	73.6	61.5	12.1	26.4	14.2	12.2	
2008............	121,328	74,363	61.3	100.0	72.2	59.3	12.9	27.8	15.0	12.8	
2009............	122,339	72,855	59.6	100.0	71.5	59.3	12.2	28.5	15.8	12.7	
2010............	123,012	71,980	58.5	100.0	71.5	59.4	12.1	28.5	15.6	12.9	
2011............	125,619	75,978	60.5	100.0	71.7	59.8	11.8	28.3	15.7	12.7	
Men											
1970............	65,296	55,041	84.3	100.0	87.6	66.1	21.5	12.4	4.4	8.0	
1975............	72,346	59,091	81.7	100.0	87.5	63.8	23.7	12.5	4.4	8.1	
1980............	80,193	64,260	80.1	100.0	87.2	65.2	22.0	12.8	4.4	8.4	
1985............	85,454	67,301	78.8	100.0	86.5	66.8	19.7	13.5	4.8	8.7	
1990	90,269	71,068	78.7	100.0	86.4	68.0	18.4	13.5	5.1	8.4	
1995............	95,867	73,667	76.8	100.0	86.2	70.6	15.6	13.9	5.5	8.4	
2000	102,853	79,446	77.2	100.0	87.5	74.2	13.3	12.6	5.5	7.1	
2005............	110,161	82,013	74.4	100.0	87.0	74.2	12.8	13.0	6.3	6.7	
2006............	111,733	83,131	74.4	100.0	87.8	75.2	12.6	12.2	5.7	6.5	
2007............	112,695	83,538	74.1	100.0	87.4	74.6	12.8	12.6	5.9	6.7	
2008............	113,758	83,109	73.1	100.0	86.0	71.2	14.8	14.0	6.5	7.5	
2009............	114,820	81,073	70.6	100.0	84.4	68.3	16.1	15.6	7.3	8.3	
2010............	115,986	80,341	69.3	100.0	84.3	69.4	14.9	15.7	7.3	8.4	
2011............	116,984	80,503	68.8	100.0	84.8	71.2	13.6	15.2	7.2	8.0	

Note: These data reflect work experience for the entire year.

Source: Annual Social and Economic Supplements, 1971–2012, Current Population Survey, U.S. Bureau of Labor Statistics.

Table 23. **Married-couple families, by number and relationship of earners, 1967–2011**

(Numbers in thousands)

Year	Married-couple families										
	Total	No earners	One earner				Two or more earners				
			Total	Husband only	Wife only	Other family member	Total	Husband and wife	Husband and other family member	Wife and other family member	Husband and wife are not earners
1967......	43,292	2,943	16,490	15,429	716	345	23,859	18,888	4,639	–	–
1968......	43,842	2,888	16,375	15,310	730	335	24,579	19,743	4,522	–	–
1969......	44,436	3,022	16,268	15,133	797	339	25,145	20,327	4,517	–	–
1970......	44,832	3,252	16,117	14,931	867	320	25,464	20,510	4,622	–	–
1971......	45,939	3,471	16,847	15,502	1,004	340	25,621	20,641	4,651	–	–
1972......	46,594	3,632	16,787	15,387	1,003	398	26,175	21,279	4,553	–	–
1973......	47,185	4,027	16,080	14,547	1,110	423	27,078	22,152	4,535	–	–
1974......	47,438	4,325	15,795	14,122	1,216	457	27,319	22,451	4,442	–	–
1975......	47,878	4,943	16,217	14,343	1,394	481	26,717	22,338	3,861	–	–
1976......	48,150	4,962	15,630	13,690	1,424	516	27,559	23,104	3,829	–	–
1977......	48,131	5,177	15,119	13,153	1,456	512	27,835	23,474	3,812	–	–
1978......	48,532	5,226	14,456	12,434	1,509	513	28,850	24,655	3,609	–	–
1979......	49,132	5,559	13,912	11,934	1,499	480	29,660	25,595	3,476	–	–
1980......	49,316	5,903	13,900	11,621	1,707	573	29,513	25,557	3,380	–	–
1981......	49,669	6,213	13,832	11,524	1,680	628	29,624	25,729	3,212	–	–
1982......	49,947	6,427	14,235	11,575	2,048	613	29,285	25,387	3,149	–	–
1983......	50,134	6,549	13,692	11,100	1,944	647	29,893	26,119	2,996	–	–
1984......	50,395	6,630	12,952	10,472	1,852	628	30,814	27,035	2,891	–	–
1985......	50,978	6,693	12,961	10,406	1,897	658	31,324	27,787	2,764	–	–
1986......	51,574	6,731	12,565	9,984	1,917	664	32,278	28,811	2,730	–	–
1987......	51,847	6,741	12,435	9,787	1,946	702	32,671	29,369	2,576	–	–
1988......	52,149	6,754	11,876	9,463	1,777	636	33,519	30,536	2,303	532	148
1989......	52,385	6,812	11,748	9,212	1,840	695	33,825	30,879	2,373	435	138
1990......	52,241	6,770	11,630	9,107	1,826	698	33,841	30,829	2,369	479	164
1991......	52,549	7,091	11,523	8,873	1,993	657	33,935	31,049	2,161	527	197
1992......	53,254	7,256	11,977	9,114	2,145	718	34,021	31,268	1,940	624	199
1993......	53,248	7,282	11,842	8,745	2,411	687	34,123	31,302	2,051	614	156
1994......	53,929	7,227	11,774	8,719	2,374	681	34,928	32,125	2,048	603	151
1995......	53,621	7,278	11,739	8,821	2,253	664	34,604	32,061	1,878	539	127
1996......	53,654	7,148	11,556	8,671	2,214	671	34,950	32,406	1,899	522	123
1997......	54,362	7,289	11,728	8,792	2,302	634	35,345	32,764	1,853	569	158
1998......	54,829	7,257	12,279	9,198	2,419	662	35,293	32,810	1,726	616	141
1999......	55,352	7,163	12,328	9,093	2,595	640	35,861	33,360	1,815	519	167
2000......	56,643	7,463	12,717	9,515	2,601	600	36,463	33,892	1,865	566	139
2001......	56,798	7,666	12,907	9,621	2,698	588	36,224	33,696	1,898	501	129
2002......	57,362	7,803	13,487	10,109	2,818	560	36,071	33,547	1,845	558	121
2003......	57,767	8,043	14,051	10,469	3,026	557	35,673	33,220	1,789	548	117
2004......	58,045	7,996	14,352	10,821	2,991	540	35,696	33,131	1,832	610	123
2005......	58,225	8,017	14,292	10,603	3,096	593	35,915	33,380	1,818	597	121
2006......	59,050	8,091	14,545	10,693	3,261	591	36,414	33,880	1,752	639	142
2007......	58,490	7,914	14,264	10,392	3,265	608	36,312	33,718	1,847	597	149
2008......	59,183	8,083	14,622	10,567	3,435	620	36,477	33,930	1,739	650	158
2009......	58,516	8,466	15,035	10,565	3,849	621	35,015	32,327	1,789	739	160
2010......	58,135	8,626	15,406	10,880	3,935	591	34,103	31,425	1,783	722	172
2011......	59,071	9,152	15,972	11,301	4,015	656	33,947	31,212	1,833	739	163

See note at end of table.

Table 23. **Married-couple families, by number and relationship of earners, 1967–2011 (continued)**

(Percent distribution)

Year	Married-couple families										
	Total	No earners	One earner				Two or more earners				
			Total	Husband only	Wife only	Other family member	Total	Husband and wife	Husband and other family member	Wife and other family member	Husband and wife are not earners
1967	100.0	6.8	38.1	35.6	1.7	0.8	55.1	43.6	10.7	–	–
1968	100.0	6.6	37.4	34.9	1.7	.8	56.1	45.0	10.3	–	–
1969	100.0	6.8	36.6	34.1	1.8	.8	56.6	45.7	10.2	–	–
1970	100.0	7.3	35.9	33.3	1.9	.7	56.8	45.7	10.3	–	–
1971	100.0	7.6	36.7	33.7	2.2	.7	55.8	44.9	10.1	–	–
1972	100.0	7.8	36.0	33.0	2.2	.9	56.2	45.7	9.8	–	–
1973	100.0	8.5	34.1	30.8	2.4	.9	57.4	46.9	9.6	–	–
1974	100.0	9.1	33.3	29.8	2.6	1.0	57.6	47.3	9.4	–	–
1975	100.0	10.3	33.9	30.0	2.9	1.0	55.8	46.7	8.1	–	–
1976	100.0	10.3	32.5	28.4	3.0	1.1	57.2	48.0	8.0	–	–
1977	100.0	10.8	31.4	27.3	3.0	1.1	57.8	48.8	7.9	–	–
1978	100.0	10.8	29.8	25.6	3.1	1.1	59.4	50.8	7.4	–	–
1979	100.0	11.3	28.3	24.3	3.1	1.0	60.4	52.1	7.1	–	–
1980	100.0	12.0	28.2	23.6	3.5	1.2	59.8	51.8	6.9	–	–
1981	100.0	12.5	27.8	23.2	3.4	1.3	59.6	51.8	6.5	–	–
1982	100.0	12.9	28.5	23.2	4.1	1.2	58.6	50.8	6.3	–	–
1983	100.0	13.1	27.3	22.1	3.9	1.3	59.6	52.1	6.0	–	–
1984	100.0	13.2	25.7	20.8	3.7	1.2	61.1	53.6	5.7	–	–
1985	100.0	13.1	25.4	20.4	3.7	1.3	61.4	54.5	5.4	–	–
1986	100.0	13.1	24.4	19.4	3.7	1.3	62.6	55.9	5.3	–	–
1987	100.0	13.0	24.0	18.9	3.8	1.4	63.0	56.6	5.0	–	–
1988	100.0	13.0	22.8	18.1	3.4	1.2	64.3	58.6	4.4	1.0	0.3
1989	100.0	13.0	22.4	17.6	3.5	1.3	64.6	58.9	4.5	.8	.3
1990	100.0	13.0	22.3	17.4	3.5	1.3	64.8	59.0	4.5	.9	.3
1991	100.0	13.5	21.9	16.9	3.8	1.3	64.6	59.1	4.1	1.0	.4
1992	100.0	13.6	22.5	17.1	4.0	1.3	63.9	58.7	3.6	1.2	.4
1993	100.0	13.7	22.2	16.4	4.5	1.3	64.1	58.8	3.9	1.2	.3
1994	100.0	13.4	21.8	16.2	4.4	1.3	64.8	59.6	3.8	1.1	.3
1995	100.0	13.6	21.9	16.5	4.2	1.2	64.5	59.8	3.5	1.0	.2
1996	100.0	13.3	21.5	16.2	4.1	1.3	65.1	60.4	3.5	1.0	.2
1997	100.0	13.4	21.6	16.2	4.2	1.2	65.0	60.3	3.4	1.0	.3
1998	100.0	13.2	22.4	16.8	4.4	1.2	64.4	59.8	3.1	1.1	.3
1999	100.0	12.9	22.3	16.4	4.7	1.2	64.8	60.3	3.3	.9	.3
2000	100.0	13.2	22.5	16.8	4.6	1.1	64.4	59.8	3.3	1.0	.2
2001	100.0	13.5	22.7	16.9	4.8	1.0	63.8	59.3	3.3	.9	.2
2002	100.0	13.6	23.5	17.6	4.9	1.0	62.9	58.5	3.2	1.0	.2
2003	100.0	13.9	24.3	18.1	5.2	1.0	61.8	57.5	3.1	.9	.2
2004	100.0	13.8	24.7	18.6	5.2	.9	61.5	57.1	3.2	1.0	.2
2005	100.0	13.8	24.5	18.2	5.3	1.0	61.7	57.3	3.1	1.0	.2
2006	100.0	13.7	24.6	18.1	5.5	1.0	61.7	57.4	3.0	1.1	.2
2007	100.0	13.5	24.4	17.8	5.6	1.0	62.1	57.6	3.2	1.0	.3
2008	100.0	13.7	24.7	17.9	5.8	1.0	61.6	57.3	2.9	1.1	.3
2009	100.0	14.5	25.7	18.1	6.6	1.1	59.8	55.2	3.1	1.3	.3
2010	100.0	14.8	26.5	18.7	6.8	1.0	58.7	54.1	3.1	1.2	.3
2011	100.0	15.5	27.0	19.1	6.8	1.1	57.5	52.8	3.1	1.3	.3

Note: Data reflect earnings and work experience for the entire year. Dash indicates data not available.

Source: Annual Social and Economic Supplements, 1968–2012, Current Population Survey, U.S. Bureau of Labor Statistics.

Table 24. **Contribution of wives' earnings to family income, 1970–2011**

Year	Contribution to family income (median percentage)
1970	26.6
1971	27.5
1972	26.7
1973	26.0
1974	25.4
1975	26.3
1976	26.4
1977	26.1
1978	26.1
1979	26.0
1980	26.7
1981	27.3
1982	28.4
1983	28.8
1984	28.4
1985	28.3
1986	29.0
1987	29.5
1988	29.6
1989	29.9
1990	30.7
1991	31.3
1992	32.4
1993	32.2
1994	31.9
1995	31.9
1996	32.6
1997	32.7
1998	32.8
1999	32.8
2000	33.5
2001	34.4
2002	34.8
2003	35.2
2004	34.9
2005	35.1
2006	35.6
2007	36.0
2008	36.0
2009	37.1
2010	37.6
2011	37.0

Note: Data reflect earnings and work experience for the entire year.

Source: Annual Social and Economic Supplements, 1971–2012, Current Population Survey, U.S. Bureau of Labor Statistics.

Table 25. **Wives who earn more than their husbands, 1987–2011**

(Numbers in thousands)

Year	Families in which wives have earnings but husbands may not[1]			Families in which both wives and husbands have earnings[2]		
	Married-couple families in which wife (but not necessarily husband) have earnings from work	Wives who earn more than their husbands	Percentage of wives who earn more than their husbands	Married-couple families in which both wife and husband have earnings from work	Wives who earn more than their husbands	Percentage of wives who earn more than their husbands
1987..............	32,025	7,581	23.7	29,755	5,311	17.8
1988..............	32,810	7,827	23.9	30,503	5,520	18.1
1989..............	33,119	8,068	24.4	30,848	5,796	18.8
1990..............	33,093	8,221	24.8	30,794	5,923	19.2
1991..............	33,516	8,983	26.8	30,998	6,465	20.9
1992..............	33,987	9,715	28.6	31,221	6,948	22.3
1993..............	34,286	10,000	29.2	31,264	6,978	22.3
1994..............	35,066	10,184	29.0	32,091	7,209	22.5
1995..............	34,819	9,822	28.2	32,030	7,033	22.0
1996..............	35,120	10,070	28.7	32,389	7,340	22.7
1997..............	35,613	10,309	28.9	32,745	7,441	22.7
1998..............	35,806	10,467	29.2	32,782	7,443	22.7
1999..............	36,454	10,548	28.9	33,340	7,434	22.3
2000..............	37,037	11,070	29.9	33,873	7,906	23.3
2001..............	36,864	11,329	30.7	33,665	8,130	24.1
2002..............	36,905	11,765	31.9	33,531	8,391	25.0
2003..............	36,761	11,923	32.4	33,189	8,351	25.2
2004..............	36,710	11,985	32.6	33,110	8,386	25.3
2005..............	37,055	12,215	33.0	33,364	8,524	25.5
2006..............	37,733	12,601	33.4	33,838	8,707	25.7
2007..............	37,536	12,570	33.5	33,678	8,712	25.9
2008..............	37,988	13,104	34.5	33,905	9,020	26.6
2009..............	36,858	13,903	37.7	32,280	9,326	28.9
2010..............	36,024	13,798	38.3	31,373	9,147	29.2
2011..............	35,908	13,505	37.6	31,165	8,762	28.1

[1] Includes families in which husband had no earnings from work.
[2] Excludes families in which husband had no earnings from work.
Note: Data reflect earnings and work experience for the entire year. Earnings include self-employment earnings.

Source: Annual Social and Economic Supplements, 1988–2012, Current Population Survey, U.S. Bureau of Labor Statistics.

Table 26. **Wage and salary workers paid hourly rates with earnings at or below the prevailing federal minimum wage, by selected characteristics, 2012 annual averages**

(Numbers in thousands)

Characteristic	Workers paid hourly rates				
	Total	Total at or below prevailing federal minimum wage			
		Total	Percentage of hourly paid workers	At prevailing federal minimum wage	Below prevailing federal minimum wage
Age and gender					
Total, 16 years and older............................	75,276	3,550	4.7	1,566	1,984
16 to 24 years...	14,909	1,797	12.1	862	935
25 years and older..................................	60,367	1,753	2.9	704	1,049
Women, 16 years and older........................	38,163	2,287	6.0	999	1,288
16 to 24 years...	7,455	1,124	15.1	529	595
25 years and older..................................	30,708	1,163	3.8	470	693
Men, 16 years and older............................	37,113	1,263	3.4	567	696
16 to 24 years...	7,454	673	9.0	333	340
25 years and older..................................	29,659	591	2.0	235	356
Race and Hispanic or Latino ethnicity					
White..	59,180	2,760	4.7	1,185	1,575
Women..	29,490	1,776	6.0	741	1,035
Men..	29,691	984	3.3	444	540
Black or African American..........................	10,049	533	5.3	277	256
Women..	5,527	350	6.3	193	157
Men..	4,522	183	4.0	85	98
Asian..	3,403	117	3.4	48	69
Women..	1,835	78	4.3	32	46
Men..	1,568	39	2.5	16	23
Hispanic or Latino	14,404	718	5.0	337	381
Women..	6,290	423	6.7	210	213
Men..	8,114	295	3.6	127	168

See footnote at end of table.

Table 26. **Wage and salary workers paid hourly rates with earnings at or below the prevailing federal minimum wage, by selected characteristics, 2012 annual averages (continued)**

(Numbers in thousands)

Characteristic	Workers paid hourly rates				
	Total	Total at or below prevailing federal minimum wage			
		Total	Percentage of hourly paid workers	At prevailing federal minimum wage	Below prevailing federal minimum wage
Full- and part-time status[1]					
Full-time workers..	54,745	1,261	2.3	501	760
Women..	24,693	770	3.1	304	466
Men...	30,052	491	1.6	197	294
Part-time workers..	20,411	2,286	11.2	1,063	1,223
Women..	13,413	1,513	11.3	693	820
Men...	6,998	772	11.0	370	402

[1] Full-time workers and those who usually work 35 or more hours per week; part-time workers are those who usually work less than 35 hours per week. Data will not sum to totals because full- or part-time status on the principal job is not identifiable for a small number of multiple jobholders.

Note: The prevailing federal minimum wage was $7.25 an hour in 2012. Data are for wage and salary workers, excluding the incorporated self-employed reflect a person's earnings on his or her sole or principal job, and pertain only to workers who are paid hourly rates. Salaried workers and other nonhourly workers are not included. Estimates for the race groups shown (White, Black or African American, and Asian) do not sum to totals because data are not presented for all races. People whose ethnicity is identified as Hispanic or Latino may be of any race.

Source: Current Population Survey, U.S. Bureau of Labor Statistics.

Table 27. **Working poor: Poverty status of people in the labor force for 27 weeks or more, by age, gender, race, and Hispanic or Latino ethnicity, 2011**

(Numbers in thousands)

Age and gender	Total					Below poverty level				
	Total	White	Black or African American	Asian	Hispanic or Latino ethnicity	Total	White	Black or African American	Asian	Hispanic or Latino ethnicity
Total, 16 years and older..........	147,475	118,070	17,330	7,825	22,503	10,382	7,175	2,299	423	2,905
16 to 19 years...................	3,263	2,612	400	113	613	370	271	76	9	109
20 to 24 years...................	13,245	10,332	1,864	448	2,731	1,855	1,245	449	43	395
25 to 34 years...................	31,907	24,688	4,096	1,934	6,236	2,989	2,048	705	99	922
35 to 44 years...................	32,029	24,987	4,011	2,091	5,841	2,307	1,612	449	126	829
45 to 54 years...................	34,625	28,049	3,969	1,774	4,467	1,765	1,185	409	100	427
55 to 64 years...................	24,583	20,664	2,330	1,164	2,097	964	703	196	41	202
65 years and older.............	7,823	6,738	660	301	516	131	111	14	4	21
Women, 16 years and older.....	69,127	54,025	9,341	3,700	9,566	5,527	3,612	1,461	199	1,309
16 to 19 years...................	1,689	1,326	223	72	270	185	128	42	7	48
20 to 24 years...................	6,400	4,895	1,001	200	1,185	1,091	709	290	22	195
25 to 34 years...................	14,632	10,947	2,220	904	2,432	1,649	1,031	497	44	425
35 to 44 years...................	14,741	11,137	2,172	965	2,473	1,157	755	280	55	355
45 to 54 years...................	16,409	13,037	2,131	850	2,004	849	540	241	44	173
55 to 64 years...................	11,897	9,846	1,259	586	962	505	371	102	22	97
65 years and older.............	3,358	2,836	336	123	241	91	77	8	4	17
Men, 16 years and older..........	78,349	64,045	7,989	4,125	12,936	4,855	3,564	838	224	1,596
16 to 19 years...................	1,574	1,286	177	41	343	185	143	34	2	62
20 to 24 years...................	6,845	5,436	863	248	1,546	764	536	159	21	201
25 to 34 years...................	17,276	13,741	1,876	1,030	3,805	1,340	1,017	208	55	497
35 to 44 years...................	17,288	13,849	1,839	1,126	3,369	1,150	857	170	71	474
45 to 54 years...................	18,215	15,012	1,839	924	2,464	916	645	168	56	254
55 to 64 years...................	12,686	10,818	1,071	578	1,135	459	332	94	19	105
65 years and older.............	4,465	3,902	323	179	275	40	34	6	–	4

See footnotes at end of table.

Table 27. **Working poor: Poverty status of people in the labor force for 27 weeks or more, by age, gender, race, and Hispanic or Latino ethnicity, 2011 (continued)**

Age and gender	Rate[1]				
	Total	White	Black or African American	Asian	Hispanic or Latino ethnicity
Total, 16 years and older.........	7.0	6.1	13.3	5.4	12.9
16 to 19 years....................	11.3	10.4	19.1	8.1	17.8
20 to 24 years....................	14.0	12.0	24.1	9.7	14.5
25 to 34 years....................	9.4	8.3	17.2	5.1	14.8
35 to 44 years....................	7.2	6.5	11.2	6.0	14.2
45 to 54 years....................	5.1	4.2	10.3	5.6	9.6
55 to 64 years....................	3.9	3.4	8.4	3.5	9.6
65 years and older..............	1.7	1.6	2.1	1.4	4.1
Women, 16 years and older......	8.0	6.7	15.6	5.4	13.7
16 to 19 years....................	10.9	9.7	18.8	([2])	17.6
20 to 24 years....................	17.0	14.5	29.0	11.2	16.4
25 to 34 years....................	11.3	9.4	22.4	4.9	17.5
35 to 44 years....................	7.8	6.8	12.9	5.7	14.3
45 to 54 years....................	5.2	4.1	11.3	5.2	8.6
55 to 64 years....................	4.2	3.8	8.1	3.8	10.0
65 years and older..............	2.7	2.7	2.5	3.1	7.1
Men, 16 years and older.........	6.2	5.6	10.5	5.4	12.3
16 to 19 years....................	11.8	11.1	19.4	([2])	17.9
20 to 24 years....................	11.2	9.9	18.4	8.4	13.0
25 to 34 years....................	7.8	7.4	11.1	5.3	13.1
35 to 44 years....................	6.7	6.2	9.2	6.3	14.1
45 to 54 years....................	5.0	4.3	9.1	6.0	10.3
55 to 64 years....................	3.6	3.1	8.8	3.2	9.3
65 years and older..............	0.9	0.9	1.7	0.1	1.4

[1] Number below the poverty level as a percentage of the total in the labor force for 27 or more weeks.

[2] Data not shown where labor force base is less than 80,000.

Note: These data reflect the earnings and work experience of the entire year. Estimates for the race groups shown (White, Black or African American, and Asian) do not sum to totals because data are not presented for all races. People whose ethnicity is identified as Hispanic or Latino may be of any race. Dash indcates estimates round to zero.

Source: 2012 Annual Social and Economic Supplement, Current Population Survey, U.S. Bureau of Labor Statistics.

Table 28. **Displaced workers[1], by age, gender, race, Hispanic or Latino ethnicity, and employment status in January 2012**

Age, gender, race, and Hispanic or Latino ethnicity	Total (in thousands)	Percentage distribution by employment status			
		Total	Employed	Unemployed	Not in labor force
Total					
Total, 20 years and older..............	6,121	100.0	56.0	26.7	17.4
20 to 24 years.........................	128	100.0	61.7	22.4	15.9
25 to 54 years.........................	4,268	100.0	61.5	26.2	12.3
55 to 64 years.........................	1,338	100.0	47.4	28.1	24.5
65 years and older.....................	386	100.0	23.5	27.5	49.0
Women, 20 years and older..........	2,681	100.0	49.7	30.8	19.5
20 to 24 years.........................	50	100.0	(2)	(2)	(2)
25 to 54 years.........................	1,831	100.0	54.6	30.9	14.5
55 to 64 years.........................	611	100.0	43.3	31.1	25.6
65 years and older.....................	189	100.0	23.5	27.7	48.8
Men, 20 years and older..............	3,440	100.0	60.9	23.4	15.7
20 to 24 years.........................	78	100.0	70.6	15.0	14.4
25 to 54 years.........................	2,438	100.0	66.7	22.7	10.6
55 to 64 years.........................	727	100.0	50.8	25.6	23.7
65 years and older.....................	197	100.0	23.5	27.3	49.2
White					
Total, 20 years and older..............	5,027	100.0	57.4	26.1	16.5
Women................................	2,107	100.0	51.2	30.2	18.7
Men....................................	2,920	100.0	61.9	23.1	14.9
Black or African American					
Total, 20 years and older..............	662	100.0	46.1	31.2	22.7
Women................................	378	100.0	41.2	35.9	22.9
Men....................................	284	100.0	52.7	24.8	22.4
Asian					
Total, 20 years and older..............	230	100.0	60.3	26.7	13.1
Women................................	109	100.0	58.9	25.6	15.5
Men....................................	121	100.0	61.5	27.6	10.9
Hispanic or Latino ethnicity					
Total, 20 years and older..............	901	100.0	54.9	27.7	17.4
Women................................	307	100.0	44.3	31.6	24.1
Men....................................	594	100.0	60.3	25.7	14.0

[1] Workers who had 3 or more years of tenure on a job they had lost or left between January 2009 and December 2011 because of plant or company closings or relocations, insufficient work, or the abolishment of their positions or shifts.

[2] Data not shown where base is less than 75,000.

Note: Estimates for the race groups shown (White, Black or African American, and Asian) do not sum to totals because data are not presented for all races. People whose ethnicity is identified as Hispanic or Latino may be of any race.

Source: January 2012 Displaced Worker Supplement to the Current Population Survey, U.S. Bureau of Labor Statistics.

Table 29. **Employed wage and salary workers, by age, gender, and median years of tenure with current employer for selected years, 1998–2012**

Age and gender	February 1998	February 2000	January 2002	January 2004	January 2006	January 2008	January 2010	January 2012
Total, 16 years and older..............	3.6	3.5	3.7	4.0	4.0	4.1	4.4	4.6
16 to 17 years..........................	.6	.6	.7	.7	.6	.7	.7	.7
18 to 19 years..........................	.7	.7	.8	.8	.7	.8	1.0	.8
20 to 24 years..........................	1.1	1.1	1.2	1.3	1.3	1.3	1.5	1.3
25 years and older....................	4.7	4.7	4.7	4.9	4.9	5.1	5.2	5.4
25 to 34 years........................	2.7	2.6	2.7	2.9	2.9	2.7	3.1	3.2
35 to 44 years........................	5.0	4.8	4.6	4.9	4.9	4.9	5.1	5.3
45 to 54 years........................	8.1	8.2	7.6	7.7	7.3	7.6	7.8	7.8
55 to 64 years........................	10.1	10.0	9.9	9.6	9.3	9.9	10.0	10.3
65 years and older....................	7.8	9.4	8.6	9.0	8.8	10.2	9.9	10.3
Women, 16 years and older..........	3.4	3.3	3.4	3.8	3.9	3.9	4.2	4.6
16 to 17 years..........................	.6	.6	.7	.6	.6	.6	.7	.7
18 to 19 years..........................	.7	.7	.8	.8	.7	.8	1.0	.8
20 to 24 years..........................	1.1	1.0	1.1	1.3	1.2	1.3	1.5	1.3
25 years and older....................	4.4	4.4	4.4	4.7	4.8	4.9	5.1	5.4
25 to 34 years........................	2.5	2.5	2.5	2.8	2.8	2.6	3.0	3.1
35 to 44 years........................	4.5	4.3	4.2	4.5	4.6	4.7	4.9	5.2
45 to 54 years........................	7.2	7.3	6.5	6.4	6.7	7.0	7.1	7.3
55 to 64 years........................	9.6	9.9	9.6	9.2	9.2	9.8	9.7	10.0
65 years and older....................	8.7	9.7	9.4	9.6	9.5	9.9	10.1	10.5
Men, 16 years and older..............	3.8	3.8	3.9	4.1	4.1	4.2	4.6	4.7
16 to 17 years..........................	.6	.6	.8	.7	.7	.7	.7	.6
18 to 19 years..........................	.7	.7	.8	.8	.7	.8	1.0	.8
20 to 24 years..........................	1.2	1.2	1.4	1.3	1.4	1.4	1.6	1.4
25 years and older....................	4.9	4.9	4.9	5.1	5.0	5.2	5.3	5.5
25 to 34 years........................	2.8	2.7	2.8	3.0	2.9	2.8	3.2	3.2
35 to 44 years........................	5.5	5.3	5.0	5.2	5.1	5.2	5.3	5.4
45 to 54 years........................	9.4	9.5	9.1	9.6	8.1	8.2	8.5	8.5
55 to 64 years........................	11.2	10.2	10.2	9.8	9.5	10.1	10.4	10.7
65 years and older....................	7.1	9.0	8.1	8.2	8.3	10.4	9.7	10.2

Source: 1998–2012 Displaced Worker Supplements to the Current Population Survey, U.S. Bureau of Labor Statistics.

Table 30. **Labor force status of 2012 high school graduates and 2011–2012 high school dropouts 16 to 24 years old, by school enrollment and gender, October 2012**

(Numbers in thousands)

Characteristic	Civilian noninsti-tutional population	Civilian labor force						Not in labor force
		Total	Percentage of population	Employed		Unemployed		
				Total	Percentage of population	Total	Percentage of labor force	
Total, 2012 high school graduates[1].........	3,203	1,563	48.8	1,161	36.3	402	25.7	1,639
Women...	1,581	781	49.4	614	38.8	167	21.4	800
Men...	1,622	783	48.2	547	33.7	235	30.0	840
Enrolled in college..............................	2,121	811	38.2	667	31.5	143	17.7	1,310
Percentage of total 2012 graduates......	66.2	51.9	–	57.5	–	35.6	–	79.9
Women...	1,127	469	41.6	395	35.1	74	15.7	658
Percentage of female 2012 graduates...	71.3	60.1	–	64.3	–	44.3	–	82.3
Men...	994	342	34.4	272	27.4	70	20.4	652
Percentage of male 2012 graduates......	61.3	43.7	–	49.7	–	29.8	–	77.6
Not enrolled in college..........................	1,082	753	69.6	494	45.7	259	34.4	329
Percentage of total 2012 graduates......	33.8	48.2	–	42.5	–	64.4	–	20.1
Women...	454	312	68.7	219	48.2	93	29.9	142
Percentage of female 2012 graduates...	28.7	39.9	–	35.7	–	55.7	–	17.8
Men...	628	441	70.2	275	43.8	166	37.5	187
Percentage of male 2012 graduates......	38.7	56.3	–	50.3	–	70.6	–	22.3
Total, 2011–2012 high school dropouts[2]...	370	174	47.2	88	23.8	86	49.6	195
Women...	178	63	35.5	28	15.9	35	(3)	115
Men...	192	111	57.9	60	31.1	52	46.3	81

[1] Data refer to persons who graduated from high school in January through October 2012.
[2] Data refer to persons who dropped out of school between October 2011 and October 2012.
[3] Data not shown where base is less than 75,000.

Note: Sums of individual items may not equal totals because of rounding.

Source: October 2012 School Enrollment Supplement to the Current Population Survey, U.S. Bureau of Labor Statistics.

Table 31. **Labor force status of persons 16 to 24 years old, by school enrollment, gender, and educational attainment, October 2012**

(Numbers in thousands)

Characteristic	Civilian noninstitutional population	Civilian labor force						Not in labor force
		Total	Percentage of population	Employed		Unemployed		
				Total	Percentage of population	Total	Percentage of labor force	
Enrolled in school............................	22,718	8,717	38.4	7,520	33.1	1,196	13.7	14,002
Women...	11,667	4,727	40.5	4,119	35.3	607	12.8	6,942
Men...	11,051	3,990	36.1	3,401	30.8	589	14.8	7,061
Enrolled in high school[1].......................	10,033	2,262	22.5	1,742	17.4	520	23.0	7,771
Women...	4,824	1,169	24.2	920	19.1	249	21.3	3,656
Men...	5,209	1,093	21.0	822	15.8	271	24.8	4,116
Enrolled in college.............................	12,685	6,454	50.9	5,778	45.6	676	10.5	6,231
Women...	6,843	3,558	52.0	3,199	46.7	358	10.1	3,286
Men...	5,842	2,897	49.6	2,579	44.2	318	11.0	2,945
Not enrolled in school.........................	16,082	12,749	79.3	10,647	66.2	2,102	16.5	3,333
Women...	7,575	5,641	74.5	4,750	62.7	891	15.8	1,934
Less than a high school diploma..........	1,135	568	50.0	405	35.6	163	28.7	568
High school graduates, no college[2].....	3,025	2,135	70.6	1,674	55.3	462	21.6	889
Some college or associate's degree....	2,112	1,715	81.2	1,526	72.2	190	11.1	397
Bachelor's degree and higher..............	1,304	1,222	93.8	1,146	87.9	76	6.2	81
Men...	8,506	7,108	83.6	5,896	69.3	1,212	17.0	1,398
Less than a high school diploma..........	1,427	1,045	73.2	744	52.1	301	28.8	382
High school graduates, no college[2].....	4,089	3,344	81.8	2,709	66.2	635	19.0	746
Some college or associate's degree....	2,043	1,830	89.5	1,625	79.5	204	11.2	214
Bachelor's degree and higher..............	946	890	94.1	818	86.5	72	8.0	56

[1] Includes a small number of people enrolled in grades below high school.
[2] Includes those who have earned a high school diploma or the equivalent.

Note: Sums of individual items may not equal totals because of rounding.

Source: October 2012 School Enrollment Supplement to the Current Population Survey, U.S. Bureau of Labor Statistics.

Table 32. **Multiple jobholders and multiple jobholding rates, by gender, 1994–2012 annual averages**

(Numbers in thousands)

Year	Total employed	Multiple jobholders				Multiple-jobholding rate[1]		
		Total	Women		Men	Total	Women	Men
			Number	Percentage of all multiple jobholders				
1994........	123,060	7,260	3,336	46.0	3,924	5.9	5.9	5.9
1995........	124,900	7,693	3,554	46.2	4,139	6.2	6.2	6.1
1996........	126,708	7,832	3,640	46.5	4,192	6.2	6.2	6.1
1997........	129,558	7,955	3,718	46.7	4,237	6.1	6.2	6.1
1998........	131,463	7,926	3,748	47.3	4,178	6.0	6.2	5.9
1999........	133,488	7,802	3,698	47.4	4,104	5.8	6.0	5.7
2000........	136,891	7,604	3,608	47.4	3,996	5.6	5.7	5.5
2001........	136,933	7,357	3,523	47.9	3,834	5.4	5.5	5.2
2002........	136,485	7,291	3,557	48.8	3,734	5.3	5.6	5.1
2003........	137,736	7,315	3,599	49.2	3,716	5.3	5.6	5.1
2004........	139,252	7,473	3,638	48.7	3,835	5.4	5.6	5.1
2005........	141,730	7,546	3,691	48.9	3,855	5.3	5.6	5.1
2006........	144,427	7,576	3,753	49.5	3,822	5.2	5.6	4.9
2007........	146,047	7,655	3,822	49.9	3,833	5.2	5.6	4.9
2008........	145,362	7,620	3,783	49.6	3,837	5.2	5.6	5.0
2009........	139,877	7,271	3,741	51.5	3,530	5.2	5.6	4.8
2010........	139,064	6,878	3,552	51.6	3,326	4.9	5.4	4.5
2011........	139,869	6,880	3,496	50.8	3,384	4.9	5.3	4.6
2012........	142,469	6,943	3,495	50.3	3,448	4.9	5.2	4.6

[1] Multiple jobholders as a percent of all employed people in specified group.

Source: Current Population Survey, U.S. Bureau of Labor Statistics.

Table 33. **Unincorporated self-employed persons in nonagricultural industries, by gender, 1976–2012 annual averages**

(Numbers in thousands)

Year	Total			Women			Men			Self-employed women as percentage of total self-employed
	Total employed	Self-employed	Self-employed as a percentage of total	Total employed	Self-employed	Self-employed as a percentage of total	Total employed	Self-employed	Self-employed as a percentage of total	
1976.....	85,421	5,782	6.8	35,027	1,549	4.4	50,394	4,233	8.4	26.8
1977.....	88,734	6,115	6.9	36,677	1,692	4.6	52,057	4,423	8.5	27.7
1978.....	92,661	6,428	6.9	38,900	1,814	4.7	53,761	4,614	8.6	28.2
1979.....	95,477	6,792	7.1	40,556	1,982	4.9	54,921	4,810	8.8	29.2
1980.....	95,938	7,001	7.3	41,461	2,097	5.1	54,477	4,904	9.0	30.0
1981.....	97,030	7,097	7.3	42,333	2,192	5.2	54,697	4,905	9.0	30.9
1982.....	96,125	7,263	7.6	42,591	2,309	5.4	53,534	4,954	9.3	31.8
1983.....	97,450	7,575	7.8	43,367	2,439	5.6	54,083	5,136	9.5	32.2
1984.....	101,685	7,785	7.7	45,262	2,566	5.7	56,423	5,219	9.2	33.0
1985.....	103,971	7,810	7.5	46,615	2,603	5.6	57,356	5,207	9.1	33.3
1986.....	106,435	7,881	7.4	48,054	2,610	5.4	58,381	5,271	9.0	33.1
1987.....	109,232	8,201	7.5	49,668	2,778	5.6	59,564	5,423	9.1	33.9
1988.....	111,800	8,519	7.6	51,020	2,955	5.8	60,780	5,564	9.2	34.7
1989.....	114,143	8,605	7.5	52,341	3,043	5.8	61,802	5,562	9.0	35.4
1990.....	115,570	8,719	7.5	53,011	3,122	5.9	62,559	5,597	8.9	35.8
1991.....	114,449	8,850	7.7	52,815	3,150	6.0	61,634	5,700	9.2	35.6
1992.....	115,246	8,576	7.4	53,380	2,963	5.6	61,866	5,613	9.1	34.5
1993.....	117,144	8,959	7.6	54,273	3,065	5.6	62,871	5,894	9.4	34.2
1994.....	119,651	9,003	7.5	55,755	3,443	6.2	63,896	5,560	8.7	38.2
1995.....	121,460	8,901	7.3	56,642	3,440	6.1	64,818	5,461	8.4	38.6
1996.....	123,264	8,971	7.3	57,630	3,506	6.1	65,634	5,465	8.3	39.1
1997.....	126,159	9,056	7.2	59,026	3,550	6.0	67,133	5,506	8.2	39.2
1998.....	128,085	8,962	7.0	59,945	3,482	5.8	68,140	5,480	8.0	38.9
1999.....	130,207	8,790	6.8	61,193	3,424	5.6	69,014	5,366	7.8	39.0
2000.....	134,427	9,205	6.8	62,983	3,631	5.8	71,444	5,573	7.8	39.4
2001.....	134,635	9,121	6.8	63,147	3,594	5.7	71,488	5,527	7.7	39.4
2002.....	134,174	8,923	6.7	62,995	3,499	5.6	71,179	5,425	7.6	39.2
2003.....	135,461	9,344	6.9	63,824	3,609	5.7	71,636	5,736	8.0	38.6
2004.....	137,020	9,467	6.9	64,182	3,607	5.6	72,838	5,860	8.0	38.1
2005.....	139,532	9,509	6.8	65,213	3,565	5.5	74,319	5,944	8.0	37.5
2006.....	142,221	9,685	6.8	66,382	3,681	5.5	75,838	6,004	7.9	38.0
2007.....	143,952	9,557	6.6	67,302	3,637	5.4	76,650	5,920	7.7	38.1
2008.....	143,194	9,219	6.4	67,358	3,483	5.2	75,836	5,736	7.6	37.8
2009.....	137,775	8,995	6.5	65,712	3,468	5.3	72,062	5,527	7.7	38.6
2010.....	136,858	8,860	6.5	65,164	3,388	5.2	71,694	5,472	7.6	38.2
2011.....	139,869	8,603	6.2	65,579	3,341	5.1	74,290	5,262	7.1	38.8
2012.....	140,283	8,749	6.2	66,353	3,483	5.2	73,930	5,266	7.1	39.8

Note: Revisions to population controls and other changes can affect the comparability of labor force levels over time. In recent years, for example, updated population controls have been introduced annually with the release of January data. Information about historical comparability is online at www.bls.gov/cps/documentation.htm#comp.

Source: Current Population Survey, U.S. Bureau of Labor Statistics.

Table 34. **Employment status of the native-born and foreign-born civilian noninstitutional population, by age and gender, 2012 annual averages**

(Numbers in thousands)

Native- or foreign-born status, age, and gender	Civilian noninsti-tutional population	Civilian labor force						Not in labor force
		Total	Percentage of population	Employed		Unemployed		
				Total	Percentage of population	Total	Percentage of labor force	
Total								
Native born[1]								
16 years and older......	205,558	129,948	63.2	119,464	58.1	10,485	8.1	75,609
16 to 24 years...........	35,059	19,379	55.3	16,202	46.2	3,177	16.4	15,680
25 to 34 years...........	33,301	27,625	83.0	25,328	76.1	2,297	8.3	5,677
35 to 44 years...........	30,932	25,737	83.2	24,058	77.8	1,679	6.5	5,195
45 to 54 years...........	36,188	28,983	80.1	27,252	75.3	1,731	6.0	7,205
55 to 64 years...........	33,297	21,377	64.2	20,189	60.6	1,189	5.6	11,919
65 years and older.....	36,780	6,847	18.6	6,435	17.5	412	6.0	29,933
Foreign born[2]								
16 years and older......	37,727	25,026	66.3	23,006	61.0	2,021	8.1	12,701
16 to 24 years...........	3,724	1,905	51.2	1,632	43.8	273	14.3	1,819
25 to 34 years...........	7,674	5,840	76.1	5,373	70.0	468	8.0	1,833
35 to 44 years...........	8,710	6,997	80.3	6,518	74.8	479	6.8	1,713
45 to 54 years...........	7,509	6,071	80.9	5,622	74.9	449	7.4	1,438
55 to 64 years...........	5,021	3,332	66.4	3,051	60.8	282	8.5	1,689
65 years and older.....	5,089	880	17.3	810	15.9	70	8.0	4,209
Women								
Native born[1]								
16 years and older......	106,579	62,046	58.2	57,251	53.7	4,795	7.7	44,533
16 to 24 years...........	17,496	9,485	54.2	8,101	46.3	1,384	14.6	8,011
25 to 34 years...........	17,012	13,129	77.2	12,070	70.9	1,059	8.1	3,883
35 to 44 years...........	15,788	12,133	76.9	11,343	71.8	790	6.5	3,655
45 to 54 years...........	18,532	13,965	75.4	13,131	70.9	834	6.0	4,567
55 to 64 years...........	17,275	10,336	59.8	9,795	56.7	540	5.2	6,940
65 years and older.....	20,476	2,998	14.6	2,811	13.7	187	6.2	17,478
Foreign born[2]								
16 years and older......	19,362	10,602	54.8	9,663	49.9	939	8.9	8,760
16 to 24 years...........	1,741	750	43.1	633	36.4	117	15.6	992
25 to 34 years...........	3,758	2,253	60.0	2,024	53.9	229	10.2	1,505
35 to 44 years...........	4,439	2,994	67.4	2,750	61.9	244	8.2	1,445
45 to 54 years...........	3,827	2,727	71.3	2,522	65.9	204	7.5	1,100
55 to 64 years...........	2,626	1,495	56.9	1,376	52.4	118	7.9	1,132
65 years and older.....	2,971	385	12.9	358	12.0	27	7.0	2,586

See footnotes at end of table.

Table 34. **Employment status of the native-born and foreign-born civilian noninstitutional population, by age and gender, 2012 annual averages (continued)**

(Numbers in thousands)

Native- or foreign-born status, age, and gender	Civilian noninsti-tutional population	Civilian labor force						Not in labor force
		Total	Percentage of population	Employed		Unemployed		
				Total	Percentage of population	Total	Percentage of labor force	
Men								
Native born[1]								
16 years and older.......	98,979	67,903	68.6	62,213	62.9	5,690	8.4	31,076
16 to 24 years...........	17,563	9,895	56.3	8,101	46.1	1,793	18.1	7,668
25 to 34 years...........	16,289	14,495	89.0	13,258	81.4	1,238	8.5	1,794
35 to 44 years...........	15,144	13,604	89.8	12,715	84.0	889	6.5	1,541
45 to 54 years...........	17,657	15,018	85.1	14,121	80.0	897	6.0	2,638
55 to 64 years...........	16,021	11,042	68.9	10,393	64.9	648	5.9	4,980
65 years and older.....	16,304	3,849	23.6	3,625	22.2	225	5.8	12,455
Foreign born[2]								
16 years and older.......	18,365	14,424	78.5	13,342	72.7	1,082	7.5	3,941
16 to 24 years...........	1,983	1,156	58.3	999	50.4	157	13.6	827
25 to 34 years...........	3,915	3,587	91.6	3,349	85.5	239	6.7	328
35 to 44 years...........	4,271	4,003	93.7	3,768	88.2	235	5.9	268
45 to 54 years...........	3,682	3,344	90.8	3,099	84.2	245	7.3	338
55 to 64 years...........	2,395	1,838	76.7	1,675	69.9	163	8.9	557
65 years and older.....	2,118	495	23.4	452	21.3	43	8.7	1,623

[1] The native born are people who were born in the United States or one of its outlying areas, such as Puerto Rico or Guam, or who were born abroad of at least one parent who was a U.S. citizen.

[2] The foreign born are those residing in the United States who were not U.S. citizens at birth. That is, they were born outside the United States or one of its outlying areas, such as Puerto Rico or Guam, to parents who were not U.S. citizens. This group includes legally admitted immigrants, refugees, students, temporary workers, and undocumented immigrants. The survey data, however, do not separately identify the number of people in these categories.

Source: Current Population Survey, U.S. Bureau of Labor Statistics.

Table 35. **Union affiliation of employed wage and salary workers, by gender, annual averages, 1983–2012**

(Numbers in thousands)

Year	Total					Women				
	Total employed	Members of unions[1]		Represented by unions[2]		Total employed	Members of unions[1]		Represented by unions[2]	
		Total	Percentage of employed	Total	Percentage of employed		Total	Percentage of employed	Total	Percentage of employed
1983......	88,290	17,717	20.1	20,532	23.3	40,433	5,908	14.6	7,262	18.0
1984.......	92,194	17,340	18.8	19,932	21.6	42,172	5,829	13.8	7,100	16.8
1985......	94,521	16,996	18.0	19,358	20.5	43,506	5,732	13.2	6,910	15.9
1986......	96,903	16,975	17.5	19,278	19.9	44,961	5,802	12.9	6,961	15.5
1987.......	99,303	16,913	17.0	19,051	19.2	46,365	5,842	12.6	6,907	14.9
1988......	101,407	17,002	16.8	19,241	19.0	47,495	5,982	12.6	7,109	15.0
1989.......	103,480	16,960	16.4	19,198	18.6	48,691	6,141	12.6	7,243	14.9
1990......	104,876	16,776	16.0	19,105	18.2	49,323	6,179	12.5	7,330	14.9
1991.......	103,723	16,612	16.0	18,790	18.1	49,105	6,142	12.5	7,247	14.8
1992......	104,668	16,418	15.7	18,578	17.7	49,842	6,274	12.6	7,411	14.9
1993......	106,101	16,627	15.7	18,682	17.6	50,626	6,516	12.9	7,610	15.0
1994......	107,989	16,748	15.5	18,850	17.5	51,419	6,642	12.9	7,740	15.1
1995......	110,038	16,360	14.9	18,346	16.7	52,369	6,430	12.3	7,479	14.3
1996.......	111,960	16,269	14.5	18,158	16.2	53,488	6,410	12.0	7,397	13.8
1997......	114,533	16,110	14.1	17,923	15.6	54,708	6,347	11.6	7,304	13.4
1998......	116,730	16,211	13.9	17,918	15.4	55,757	6,362	11.4	7,280	13.1
1999......	118,963	16,477	13.9	18,182	15.3	57,050	6,528	11.4	7,425	13.0
2000......	122,089	16,334	13.4	18,153	14.9	58,427	6,671	11.4	7,662	13.1
2001......	122,229	16,305	13.3	18,026	14.7	58,582	6,768	11.6	7,672	13.1
2002......	121,826	16,145	13.3	17,695	14.5	58,555	6,820	11.6	7,629	13.0
2003......	122,358	15,776	12.9	17,448	14.3	59,122	6,732	11.4	7,601	12.9
2004......	123,554	15,472	12.5	17,087	13.8	59,408	6,593	11.1	7,450	12.5
2005......	125,889	15,685	12.5	17,223	13.7	60,423	6,815	11.3	7,626	12.6
2006......	128,237	15,359	12.0	16,860	13.1	61,426	6,702	10.9	7,501	12.2
2007......	129,767	15,670	12.1	17,243	13.3	62,299	6,903	11.1	7,749	12.4
2008......	129,377	16,098	12.4	17,761	13.7	62,532	7,160	11.4	8,036	12.9
2009......	124,490	15,327	12.3	16,904	13.6	60,951	6,887	11.3	7,727	12.7
2010......	124,073	14,715	11.9	16,290	13.1	60,542	6,722	11.1	7,528	12.4
2011......	125,187	14,764	11.8	16,290	13.0	60,502	6,758	11.2	7,558	12.5
2012......	127,577	14,366	11.3	15,922	12.5	61,679	6,470	10.5	7,311	11.9

See footnotes at end of table.

Table 35. **Union affiliation of employed wage and salary workers, by gender, annual averages, 1983–2012 (continued)**

(Numbers in thousands)

Year	Total employed	Men			
		Members of unions[1]		Represented by unions[2]	
		Total	Percentage of employed	Total	Percentage of employed
1983......	47,856	11,809	24.7	13,270	27.7
1984.......	50,022	11,511	23.0	12,832	25.7
1985......	51,015	11,264	22.1	12,448	24.4
1986......	51,942	11,173	21.5	12,317	23.7
1987.......	52,938	11,071	20.9	12,144	22.9
1988......	53,912	11,019	20.4	12,132	22.5
1989......	54,789	10,820	19.7	11,955	21.8
1990......	55,553	10,597	19.1	11,775	21.2
1991.......	54,618	10,470	19.2	11,542	21.1
1992......	54,826	10,144	18.5	11,167	20.4
1993......	55,475	10,112	18.2	11,072	20.0
1994......	56,570	10,106	17.9	11,110	19.6
1995......	57,669	9,929	17.2	10,868	18.8
1996.......	58,473	9,859	16.9	10,761	18.4
1997......	59,825	9,763	16.3	10,619	17.7
1998......	60,973	9,850	16.2	10,638	17.4
1999......	61,914	9,949	16.1	10,758	17.4
2000......	63,662	9,664	15.2	10,491	16.5
2001......	63,647	9,538	15.0	10,354	16.3
2002......	63,272	9,325	14.7	10,066	15.9
2003......	63,236	9,044	14.3	9,848	15.6
2004......	64,145	8,878	13.8	9,638	15.0
2005......	65,466	8,870	13.5	9,597	14.7
2006......	66,811	8,657	13.0	9,360	14.0
2007......	67,468	8,767	13.0	9,494	14.1
2008......	66,846	8,938	13.4	9,724	14.5
2009......	63,539	8,441	13.3	9,176	14.4
2010......	63,531	7,994	12.6	8,761	13.8
2011......	64,686	8,006	12.4	8,731	13.5
2012......	65,898	7,895	12.0	8,611	13.1

[1] Members of a labor union or an employee association similar to a union.

[2] Members of a labor union or an employee association similar to a union, as well as workers who are not members of unions but whose jobs are covered by a union or employee association contract.

Note: Data refer to the sole or principal job of full- and part-time workers. All self-employed workers are excluded, regardless of whether their businesses are or are not incorporated. Revisions to population controls and other changes can affect the comparability of labor force levels over time. In recent years, for example, updated population controls have been introduced annually with the release of January data. Information about historical comparability is online at www.bls.gov/cps/documentation.htm#comp.

Source: Current Population Survey, U.S. Bureau of Labor Statistics.

Table 36. **Employment status of persons 18 years and over, by veteran status, period of service, and gender, 2012 annual averages**

(Numbers in thousands)

Employment status and period of service	Total	Women	Men	Women as a percentage of total
Total veterans, 18 years of age and older				
Civilian noninstitutional population.............................	21,183	1,815	19,368	8.6
Civilian labor force...	11,006	1,122	9,884	10.2
Participation rate..	52.0	61.8	51.0	
Employed..	10,233	1,029	9,204	10.1
Employment-population ratio............................	48.3	56.7	47.5	
Unemployed..	773	93	680	12.0
Unemployment rate...................................	7.0	8.3	6.9	
Not in labor force...	10,177	693	9,484	6.8
Period of service				
Gulf War-era II veterans				
Civilian noninstitutional population.............................	2,566	431	2,136	16.8
Civilian labor force...	2,071	297	1,774	14.3
Participation rate..	80.7	68.9	83.1	
Employed..	1,866	259	1,606	13.9
Employment-population ratio............................	72.7	60.2	75.2	
Unemployed..	205	37	168	18.0
Unemployment rate...................................	9.9	12.5	9.5	
Not in labor force...	496	134	362	27.0
Gulf War-era I veterans				
Civilian noninstitutional population.............................	3,049	482	2,567	15.8
Civilian labor force...	2,548	364	2,184	14.3
Participation rate..	83.6	75.5	85.1	
Employed..	2,398	335	2,063	14.0
Employment-population ratio............................	78.6	69.5	80.4	
Unemployed..	150	29	121	19.3
Unemployment rate...................................	5.9	8.0	5.6	
Not in labor force...	501	118	383	23.6
World War II, Korean War, and Vietnam-era veterans				
Civilian noninstitutional population.............................	9,872	318	9,554	3.2
Civilian labor force...	3,165	102	3,063	3.2
Participation rate..	32.1	32.1	32.1	
Employed..	2,964	98	2,866	3.3
Employment-population ratio............................	30.0	30.7	30.0	
Unemployed..	201	4	197	2.0
Unemployment rate...................................	6.4	4.1	6.4	
Not in labor force...	6,707	216	6,491	3.2

See note at end of table.

Table 36. **Employment status of persons 18 years and over, by veteran status, period of service, and gender, 2012 annual averages (continued)**

(Numbers in thousands)

Employment status and period of service	Total	Women	Men	Women as a percentage of total
Veterans of other service periods				
Civilian noninstitutional population................................	5,696	584	5,112	10.3
Civilian labor force..	3,222	359	2,863	11.1
Participation rate..	56.6	61.5	56.0	
Employed...	3,006	337	2,669	11.2
Employment-population ratio................................	52.8	57.7	52.2	
Unemployed..	217	22	194	10.1
Unemployment rate..	6.7	6.2	6.8	
Not in labor force..	2,473	225	2,248	9.1
Nonveterans, 18 years and older				
Civilian noninstitutional population................................	213,211	119,785	93,425	56.2
Civilian labor force..	142,017	70,524	71,493	49.7
Participation rate..	66.6	58.9	76.5	
Employed...	130,817	65,125	65,692	49.8
Employment-population ratio................................	61.4	54.4	70.3	
Unemployed..	11,200	5,399	5,801	48.2
Unemployment rate..	7.9	7.7	8.1	
Not in labor force..	71,194	49,261	21,933	69.2

Note: Veterans served on active duty in the U.S. Armed Forces and were not on active duty at the time of the survey. Veterans could have served anywhere in the world during these periods of service: Gulf War era II (September 2001 to present), Gulf War era I (August 1990-August 2001), Vietnam era (August 1964 to April 1975), Korean War (July 1950 to January 1955), World War II (December 1941 to December 1946), and other service periods (all other time periods). Veterans who served in more than one wartime period are classified only in the most recent one. Veterans who served during one of the selected wartime periods and another period are classified only in the wartime period.

Source: Current Population Survey, U.S. Bureau of Labor Statistics.

Table 37. **Employment and disability status of persons, by gender and age, 2012 annual averages**

(Numbers in thousands)

Employment status and age	Total	Women	Men
Total persons with a disability, 16 years and older			
Civilian noninstitutional population	28,251	15,322	12,929
Civilian labor force	5,816	2,626	3,190
Participation rate	20.6	17.1	24.7
Employed	5,037	2,267	2,770
Employment-population ratio	17.8	14.8	21.4
Unemployed	779	359	420
Unemployment rate	13.4	13.7	13.2
Not in labor force	22,435	12,696	9,739
16 to 64 years			
Civilian noninstitutional population	15,339	7,775	7,564
Civilian labor force	4,854	2,249	2,605
Participation rate	31.6	28.9	34.4
Employed	4,146	1,918	2,228
Employment-population ratio	27.0	24.7	29.5
Unemployed	708	331	377
Unemployment rate	14.6	14.7	14.5
Not in labor force	10,484	5,525	4,959
65 years and older			
Civilian noninstitutional population	12,912	7,547	5,365
Civilian labor force	961	377	585
Participation rate	7.4	5.0	10.9
Employed	890	349	542
Employment-population ratio	6.9	4.6	10.1
Unemployed	71	28	43
Unemployment rate	7.4	7.4	7.3
Not in labor force	11,951	7,171	4,780
Total persons without a disability, 16 years and older			
Civilian noninstitutional population	215,034	110,619	104,415
Civilian labor force	149,159	70,022	79,137
Participation rate	69.4	63.3	75.8
Employed	137,433	64,647	72,785
Employment-population ratio	63.9	58.4	69.7
Unemployed	11,727	5,375	6,352
Unemployment rate	7.9	7.7	8.0
Not in labor force	65,875	40,597	25,278

See note at end of table.

Table 37. **Employment and disability status of persons, by gender and age, 2012 annual averages (continued)**

(Numbers in thousands)

Employment status and age	Total	Women	Men
16 to 64 years			
Civilian noninstitutional population..............................	186,077	94,719	91,358
Civilian labor force..	142,393	67,016	75,377
Participation rate..	76.5	70.8	82.5
Employed...	131,078	61,827	69,251
Employment-population ratio..............................	70.4	65.3	75.8
Unemployed..	11,315	5,189	6,127
Unemployment rate..	7.9	7.7	8.1
Not in labor force..	43,683	27,703	15,980
65 years and older			
Civilian noninstitutional population..............................	28,957	15,900	13,057
Civilian labor force..	6,766	3,006	3,760
Participation rate..	23.4	18.9	28.8
Employed...	6,355	2,820	3,535
Employment-population ratio..............................	21.9	17.7	27.1
Unemployed..	411	186	225
Unemployment rate..	6.1	6.2	6.0
Not in labor force..	22,191	12,894	9,297

Note: A person with a disability has at least one of the following conditions: deaf or serious difficulty hearing; blind or serious difficulty seeing even when wearing glasses; serious difficulty concentrating, remembering, or making decisions because of a physical, mental, or emotional condition; serious difficulty walking or climbing stairs; difficulty dressing or bathing; or difficulty doing errands alone, such as visiting a doctor's office or shopping, because of a physical, mental, or emotional condition.

Source: Current Population Survey, U.S. Bureau of Labor Statistics.

Technical Notes

The estimates in this report were obtained from the Current Population Survey (CPS), a national monthly sample survey of approximately 60,000 eligible households that provides a wide range of information on the labor force, employment, and unemployment. The survey is conducted for the U.S. Bureau of Labor Statistics (BLS) by the U.S. Census Bureau, using a scientifically selected national sample with coverage in all 50 states and the District of Columbia.

Material in this report is in the public domain and, with appropriate credit, may be reproduced without permission. This information is available upon request to individuals with sensory impairments. Voice phone: (202) 691-5200; Federal Relay Service: (800) 877-8339.

Concepts and Definitions

Civilian noninstitutional population. Included are people 16 years of age and older residing in any of the 50 states or the District of Columbia who are not confined to institutions, such as nursing homes and prisons, and who are not on active duty in the Armed Forces.

Civilian labor force. This group comprises all people classified as employed or unemployed.

Civilian labor force participation rate. This rate is the civilian labor force as a percentage of the civilian noninstitutional population.

Employed people. Employed people are all those who, during the survey reference week, (a) did any work at all as paid employees; (b) worked in their own business, in a profession, or on their own farm; or (c) worked 15 or more hours as unpaid workers in a family member's business. People who were temporarily absent from their jobs or business because of illness, vacation, a labor dispute, or another reason also are counted as employed.

Employment–population ratio. This ratio is the number of employed as a percentage of the population.

Unemployed. The unemployed are people who had no employment during the survey reference week, were available for work (except in the case of temporary illness), and had made specific efforts to find employment sometime during the 4-week period ending with the survey reference week. People who were waiting to be recalled to a job from which they had been laid off need not have been looking for work to be classified as unemployed.

Unemployment rate. This rate is the number of unemployed people as a percentage of the civilian labor force.

Not in the labor force. Included in this group are all people in the civilian noninstitutional population who are neither employed nor unemployed. People marginally attached to the labor force are those individuals not in the labor force who wanted and were available for work and had looked for a job sometime in the prior 12 months (or since the end of their last job if they held one within the past 12 months). These people were not counted as unemployed because they had not searched for work in the 4 weeks preceding the survey. Discouraged workers, a subset of the marginally attached, were not looking for work because they believed that no jobs were available for them.

Race. In accordance with the Office of Management and Budget guidelines, White, Black or African American, and Asian are terms used to describe a person's race. Beginning in 2003, people in these categories are those who selected that race group only. Those who identify multiple race groups are categorized as people of two or more races. (Previously, people identified a group as their main race.) In the enumeration process, race is determined by the household respondent. More information on the 2003 changes to questions on race and Hispanic ethnicity is available at **http://www.bls.gov/cps/rvcps03.pdf**.

Hispanic or Latino ethnicity. This refers to people who identified themselves in the enumeration process as being Hispanic, Latino, or Spanish. People whose ethnicity is identified as Hispanic or Latino may be of any race; estimates for the race groups include Hispanics. More information on the 2003 changes in questions on race and

Hispanic ethnicity is available at **http://www.bls.gov/cps/ rvcps03.pdf**.

Family. A family is a group of two or more people residing together who are related by birth, marriage, or adoption; all such people are considered as members of one family. Families are classified either as married-couple families or as families maintained by women or men without spouses present. Families include those without children as well as those with children under 18.

Children. Data on children refer to one's own children and include sons, daughters, stepchildren, and adopted children. Not included are nieces, nephews, grandchildren, other related children, and all unrelated children living in the household.

Self-employed workers. Self-employed workers are those who work for profit or fees in their own business, in a profession, in a trade, or on a farm. The unincorporated self-employed are included in the self-employed category. Self-employed people whose businesses are incorporated are included with wage and salary workers.

Wage and salary workers. These are workers who receive wages, salaries, commissions, tips, payment in kind, or piece rates. The group includes employees in the private and the public sectors. Data on union membership and earnings of wage and salary workers exclude all self-employed workers, both those with incorporated businesses and those with unincorporated businesses.

Workers paid by the hour. These are people paid at an hourly rate on their main job. Historically, workers paid an hourly wage have made up approximately three-fifths of all wage and salary workers.

Usual weekly earnings. Data on usual weekly earnings represent earnings before taxes and other deductions, and include any overtime pay, commissions, and tips usually received (at the main job in the case of multiple jobholders). Earnings reported on a basis other than weekly (e.g., annual, monthly, or hourly) are converted to weekly. The term "usual" is as perceived by the respondent. If the respondent asks for a definition of "usual," interviewers are instructed to define the term as "more than half the weeks

worked during the past 4 or 5 months." Data refer to the sole or primary job of wage and salary workers (excluding all self-employed people, regardless of whether their businesses were incorporated) and are tabulated from one-quarter of the CPS monthly sample.

Median weekly earnings. These figures indicate the number that divides the earnings distribution into two equal parts, one part having values above the median and the other having values below the median. Median weekly earnings shown in this publication are estimated through the linear interpolation of the $50-centered interval in which the median lies.

Minimum wage. The estimates of the numbers of workers with reported earnings at or below the federal minimum wage pertain only to workers who are paid hourly rates. Salaried workers and other workers who are not paid by the hour are not included, even though some have earnings that, if converted to hourly rates, would be at or below the minimum wage. Consequently, the estimates presented in this report likely understate the actual number of workers with hourly earnings at or below the minimum wage. BLS does not routinely estimate the hourly earnings of workers not paid by the hour, because of data quality concerns associated with such an estimation process.

The prevailing federal minimum wage is $7.25, effective July 24, 2009. Note that some states have established minimum-wage standards that exceed the federal level. The presence of workers with hourly earnings below the minimum wage does not necessarily indicate violations of the Fair Labor Standards Act (FLSA), because there are a number of exemptions to the minimum-wage provisions of the law. In addition, some workers might have rounded their hourly earnings in response to survey questions. As a result, some might have reported hourly earnings below the minimum wage when, in fact, they earned the minimum wage or higher.

Hours at work. These are the actual hours worked (at all jobs) during the survey reference week. For example, people who normally work 40 hours a week but were off during the Columbus Day holiday would be reported as working 32 hours, even if they were paid for the holiday.